CHAMPIONS UPRISING

REVIEWS

"Chris Romulo is a mix of heart and grit. And *Champions Uprising* is the perfect example of determination. It will motivate you to get up, no matter how hard you've been knocked down—in or out of the ring. Warning: this book will inspire you."

- Nathan Aripez, MuayThaiAuthority.com

"Much like his bouts in the ring, Romulo's unflinching head-on approach to tough truths, wins, and losses alike can break your heart and build you up within just a few passages. You don't have to know what it is to face an opponent in the ring to relate to his journey. Everyone can stand to 'Champ Up' and realize their dreams."

- Tari Ayala, Managing Editor, Money Magazine

"The parallels between Chris' ring fights and the battles he fought in life are something anyone can relate to. This book is about family; it's about losing it all, and then coming back stronger. It's a must read for anyone wanting to be a champion in life."

-Jay Hernandez, Player Development, Orlando Magic

"Chris Romulo is the personification of what it takes to be a champion - not just in the ring, but in life. No matter how many hits he takes, he just keeps moving forward. And in this book, Chris's story and advice will inspire you to keep moving forward too. Read it. Today."

- Ryan Lee, Founder of Freedym.com

"Chris' story is truly amazing. It shows what having heart and perseverance is all about. His story is a reminder that through hard work and determination, anything is possible."

- Jason Strout, Striking Coach

CHAMPIONS UPRISING

Fall 7 Times, Stand Up 8

A Memoir

By Chris Romulo and John Wolcott

ISBN-10: 1546469834
ISBN-13: 978-1546469834

To my parents, who showed me the way.

CONTENTS

FOREWORD

T he first time I heard about Chris Romulo, I was told he was a former Muay Thai fighter. I didn't know what Muay Thai was, so I went online and watched him compete. I've been a boxing fan my entire life. I love boxing. I watched the big Ali fights, the Frazier fights, the Holmes fights, the Norton fights, and the Tyson fights. I believed I wasn't only a fight fan, but that I understood fighting. And the second I saw Chris Romulo in the ring, I didn't know a ballerina could box. It was something so pure and innocent but at the same time so vicious. Chris was so prepared for war, so prepared for battle, so focused on competing and winning. But he did it in such a fluid and nonthreatening way. Watching him took my breath away and at that moment I knew I needed to meet Chris.

Chris and I have a lot in common. We've both overcome a lot. I've reached a lot of my professional goals. But I don't know if I've achieved what Chris has achieved. There are few people who can go in the ring and use their elbows, their knees, their fists, their feet, and do it at a level so extreme, that one shot from your opponent can kill you. That's a level I'll never be able to obtain. And the understanding and preparedness to do battle—it isn't just being a warrior. It's something greater. I don't understand it. But the preparation that goes into that kind of battle is all-encompassing. It's eating. It's breathing. It's working out. It's lifting. It's fighting. But more importantly, it's a mental strength few people have.

Chris has been able to take his adversity and his demons, and funnel them into something that made him a champion. And he needed to become a champion. He needed to focus and force that out of his body. And once he did he was able to help other people. He's helped more people in the last several years than I'll ever help in a lifetime. And he does it in a real way. Whether it's a five-year-old kickboxing with him, or whether it's a former champion sparring with him, he gives you the same attention. He makes you feel like you're the only person in the world, and the only person in the gym.

I don't understand a champion's mindset. I don't

understand a champion's spirit. But when I'm in the presence of Chris Romulo, I feel it. And I get closer to understanding it. That doesn't mean Chris doesn't have flaws. That doesn't mean Chris doesn't have weaknesses. That doesn't mean Chris doesn't have moments. But Chris has done something consistently for over twenty years, and he's done it at the highest level. Now Chris and his wife, Sarah, have built themselves an incredible gym that has not only helped them, but also helped the community. And every single day he's in the gym fighting the fight. And every single day I see little kids, I see middle-aged people, I see older people, looking up to him. And isn't that what life is about?

This book isn't about overcoming. This book isn't about being a champion. This is a book about consistency. This is a book about focus. This is a book about energy and understanding how to take that and be a better person every single day. But this book is also about instilling the warrior spirit and the champion spirit that I'm still trying to find, and that I'm trying to learn from Chris. There needs to be more Chris Romulo's on this Earth. I'm a better person for knowing Chris Romulo.

Anthony Melchiorri
Host of *Hotel Impossible*
Rockaway Beach, NY, April 26, 2017

BEFORE THE OPENING BELL

PROLOGUE
CHAMPIONS UPRISING

"Out of suffering have emerged the strongest souls; the most massive
characters are seared with scars."
- Khalil Gibran

I've been involved in Muay Thai for the past twenty years, fighting for the longest running fight promotion in New York City, Friday Night Fights, and teaching, most recently, what I've learned over those twenty years to members, both young and old, of the Rockaway Beach community in Far Rockaway, New York. Along with my wife, Sarah, we've run five gyms in Rockaway Beach since 2010. Our current gym is the five thousand square foot, CROM Physical Culture. And it's the culmination of the successes and setbacks we've faced over the last seven years.

My life, though, was shaped long before Muay Thai and a long way from the shorelines of Rockaway Beach, in the neighborhood of Queens Village. Growing up, Queens Village—or The Ville as we called it—was a place of corner bodegas and churches, of liquor stores and beauty salons, and of gritty New York City life that played out on what seemed like the only place I knew—Two Hundred and Eighth Street and Ninetieth Avenue. The Ville was also a place of diversity, where African American, Caribbean, and Latino immigrants settled for a better life. But the melting pot, at times, stirred plenty of controversy. And to survive in The Ville, you had to be tough, independent, and street smart.

My father, Carlito, immigrated to New York in 1970 from Manila, the capital of the Philippines. For as far back as I could remember he worked as an orderly at Hempstead General Hospital in Hempstead, New York. On Wednesdays, my brothers and I would go with him to pick up his paycheck. And on the way back home we'd stop at McDonald's to get burgers. It's one of the few memories I have of my father doing anything with us. Because most of the time he sat at the kitchen table writing lottery numbers: the numbers he played, the numbers he hadn't yet played, the numbers that might hit, the numbers that did hit. My father was, and still is, a lifelong gambler. And although his addiction to gambling kept him disconnected from the family, watching him obsess over numbers taught me about passion, dedication, and focus; passion, because he gambled with fervor; dedication, because he never quit; and focus, because more often than not he buried himself in lottery numbers, never once raising his head to acknowledge his family.

My mother, Lucita, immigrated to New York from the poverty-stricken Northeastern region of the Philippines in 1966. She had dreams of becoming a schoolteacher but put her life on hold to support her family. For most of her adult life she worked as a pharmacist's technician, sending what money she could back to her mother in the Philippines. My mother would come home complaining about incompetent coworkers and having to pick up their slack. She stuck it out, though, and worked with integrity. But because she never pursued her dreams, she carried with her a deep-seated anger for life. My mother also devoted herself to the Catholic faith, like many Filipinos. But she relinquished control over her life. Whatever happened, she said, was God's will. Just as my father had taught me in some twisted way about passion and dedication and focus from gambling, my mother taught me about hard work and integrity. Because I saw what my mom went through, I never wanted to spend my life confined to a soul sucking nine-to-five. And I would never, as long as I live, put my faith in anyone other than myself. I wanted to carve my own path.

I have two younger brothers as well, Andrew and Joey. And my mother and father worked hard to Americanize us. They didn't teach us Tagalog, the main language of the Philippines. They didn't feed us traditional Filipino foods, like afritada. And unlike so many of my friends, whose parents also immigrated to The Ville, we never visited our motherland. I had neighborhood friends who went back to their home country to see relatives. I was envious they got away from Queens and saw the world. Later on in life, when I started dating, I never understood when my mom would tell me to find a nice Filipino girl. Her and my father had done such an efficient job at Americanizing us that I never felt connected to Filipino culture. I instead connected myself to the culture of inner city Queens, New York, listening to hip-hop groups like Das EFX and following the legendary life of Bruce Lee.

But in a lot of ways, like my father, I disconnected myself from life and from family. During my formative years I kept to myself and avoided conflict. One time, at seven years old, I was playing a game of ball in the schoolyard at recess. I had a disagreement with another kid and he jumped at me. I felt the thud of his fist against my chest. I never was hit before and didn't know how to react. When I looked down I realized he didn't hit me, he stabbed me with a pencil. So I stood there, with the pencil lodged in the meat of my chest, not knowing what to do. I pulled the pencil out of my chest and went about my day as if nothing happened. I didn't tell my teachers. I didn't tell my mom or dad. And I never confronted the kid about the incident. To this day I still have the lead in the flesh of my chest as a reminder of the passivity that shadowed my youth.

When my family lived in Elmhurst Queens I made good grades and took interest in my studies. I even made the honor roll. But when we moved to Queens Village everything changed. In the fourth grade I had a public school teacher, Mr. B., who reminded me of Penguin from *Batman* because he wobbled around class with his glasses and polyester pants and short-sleeve button down shirt. Spit would collect on the side of his mouth. And when he yelled at me saliva sprayed everywhere. But Mr. B. didn't only verbally abuse me. When he was mad, he grabbed and twisted my skin, breaking the flesh or leaving bruises. I couldn't tell my mom because she always thought I deserved what happened to me— good or bad. And she wouldn't understand anyway. In her time, physical punishment existed in the Philippines. But if I had any doubts about whether or not I liked school, Mr. B. helped me answer the question. Because of his abuse, I retreated into a shell and my grades dropped.

I was the only Asian kid in a black and Latino school so I was bullied a lot. Kids called me chink. I was muscled around and pushed off the basketball court. At lunchtime kids knocked the food tray out of my hands. And in the hallways they tripped me. Eventually, I was fed up with everything and started hanging out with the kids who bullied me. I thought if I hung around with them and did what they did, they'd accept me. I began to bully kids, and for once, I felt good about myself. My actions worked at school. But they destroyed my life at home.

My brother, Joey, who was ten years younger than me, was safe from my bouts of anger. But my brother, Andrew, who was closer to my age, wasn't. I resented Andrew because he had a new girl in his life all the time. And he didn't have the same toughness I had. So I bullied him. One day he was playing video games in the house with his friend and they started to argue. I told them not to argue but they continued to bicker. So I punched Andrew in the stomach. My brother dropped to the floor, curled up in a ball, and howled in agony. His friend ran out of the house. When my parents came home they took my brother to the hospital, and luckily, nothing serious happened. But as much as I manhandled my brother I loved him the same, in the only way I knew how—with tough love.

Whenever Andrew had problems at school I showed up and took care of it for him. And if I couldn't be there for him, I gave him advice on what to do. I wanted Andrew to hold his own. So when he had a falling out with his friend from the neighborhood, I arranged for them to shoot the fair one—that's what we called fighting back in the day, because no one would jump in. Before the fight I took my brother aside and showed him how to grapple and dirty box. During the scrap he did what I showed him, but he started to lose. A few kids who were watching wanted to step in and break up the fight. But I told them to let Andrew figure it out by himself.

Over the last twenty years, though, my philosophies on life have changed. My relationship with my brother has improved in ways I would've never imagined. We now turn to each other for advice on life, business, and fatherhood. And my relationship with my mother has improved. Despite not following the path she wanted me to walk, she's more accepting of who I've become. My father, on the other hand, remains a closed book. As much as I tried over the years to crack his shell and get him to open up, I've been unsuccessful. And this has caused a great challenge for me as a man, as a son, and as a father of two boys.

Over the years I've been beaten, but I've experienced the triumph of return. I've been abandoned, but I've embraced. I've lost, but I've also gained. And where my heart was once closed off from the world, it has been opened. I always wanted to do something bigger with my life, something greater than what I witnessed my mother and father and friends from my neighborhood do with theirs. Not that I was better than any of them, but I wasn't content. My mother put her faith in religion. She put her faith in the salvation of the nine-to-five. And my father put his faith in gambling. He took the path of least resistance, relying on hope and luck. Since I couldn't put my faith in either my mother or father, I put faith in myself. I didn't rely on external sources for strength. I didn't rely on hope or luck or shy away from resistance. Instead, I faced adversity head on and worked to improve myself.

Improvement didn't come easy, though. I walked away from situations when I should've acted. And I acted when I should've walked away. I never knew how to make the right choices. And I never had anyone to turn to for guidance. So I found myself turning to the streets, to self-destruction, to violence. I made bad judgment calls, one nearly costing my life. It took a lot of trial and error before I figured out how to cultivate the champion's spirit. And until I had enough skill to rise up against the voices of fear and doubt, much strife followed. But I've grown and learned from my mistakes. And I was able to transform my experiences into valuable lessons; lessons I believe will help you along your journey through life.

But to say my successes are my own doing would be inaccurate, because people have come in and out of my life and changed me in positive ways. Some of these people you'll read about in this book, others I carry with me in my heart, like Kevin Murphy and Anthony Melchiorri.

I trained Kevin Murphy while I worked at New York Sports Club. He played college football and had dreams of going to the NFL. But he suffered an injury and instead turned his passion toward business. Kevin became my first financial mentor and taught me not everyone with money is evil, which was the consensus growing up in a poor neighborhood. I saw the good Kevin did for people—me being one of them—and I wanted the financial freedom to do the same.

Anthony Melchiorri, another client of mine, has also been a

mentor, a friend, and like family to my wife, Sarah, and me since 2013. Anthony is the host of *Hotel Impossible* on the Travel Channel. I met Anthony at a time in my life when I thought Sarah and I were back on our feet. But Anthony showed us how to step out of our comfort zone and go bigger. He sees more in us than we see in ourselves. And his vision helped expand our vision. And if not for his belief in us, I'm not sure where we'd be today.

You might think fighters are special breeds, and in some ways we are. But I believe there's nothing I did in my life that you can't do. But it takes change—change of action, change of environment, change of people, and most importantly, change of mindset.

Champions Uprising is the story of my change. It's the story of how I transformed myself from a misguided kid running the streets of Queens into a professional Muay Thai champion. *Champions Uprising* is the story about my journey through martial arts and how Muay Thai helped me overcome life's greatest threats and challenges. But *Champions Uprising* is also a story about choices and relationships. Because the choices we make not only impact us, but those closest to us.

I want to share my story so you, too, can recognize the champion within. Because if someone like me can go from living in scarcity to living with purpose, so can you. The stories that follow are mine. The lessons I've learned are universal. I hope each story inspires you to reflect on and change your life the way they've helped me change mine. I hope each story helps you find the message of your life. And I hope by the end of this book you've not only experienced my champion's uprising, but you've begun to recognize your own.

ROUND ONE: TIMING IS EVERYTHING

CHAPTER ONE
THE FIGHT THAT CHANGED EVERYTHING

"All it takes is heart."
- Chris Romulo

Growing up in The Ville, life was about having a rep on the streets. I wanted to be the toughest guy on the block. Or be part of the toughest crew in the neighborhood. I wanted people to hear the Romulo name and show respect. One evening, as the sun came down over Queens, my boy Pat and I took a walk down Jamaica Avenue to buy a few beers from the bodega. As we came to the corner of Two Hundred and Tenth Street and Jamaica Avenue a bus rolled to a stop in front of us. The rear doors folded open and a kid in a hoodie and baggy jeans and Timberlands stepped onto the sidewalk. We recognized him as Edwin, one of the guys from a rival neighborhood in Hollis, Queens.

Edwin's family migrated from Haiti to Queens to escape the political repression of their home country. Like many other Haitian immigrants, his family sought out New York City for a more peaceful way of life, a life that afforded opportunity. But along the way Edwin got sucked into the streets. As a teenager he spent time in juvenile detention centers. And as a young adult he did time in Rikers Island. And a few weeks before seeing him at the bus stop, Pat fought his boy, Jungle, who got his nickname from biting people in street fights. Expecting Edwin to do something, I kept my eye on him as we neared each other.

Edwin walked by us and looked up. We locked eyes. I didn't want to be the first to look away, because that would mean Edwin punked me. And my ego wouldn't let that happen. I turned my head to follow his eyes as he passed me. "Whatchew looking at?" I said. He replied with the same snarky question. When you grow up on the streets there's explicit language and there's implicit language. Both of us understood those words implied, "Do you want to fight?"

I threw my hands plenty of times. If I took out Edwin, I thought, I could further my name on the streets. I slid my arms out of my Penn State Starter jacket and dropped it on the sidewalk. Edwin did the same. We put our hands up and circled each other. And we started to scrap on Jamaica Avenue.

As we tussled Edwin showed his fighting abilities. I had trouble getting my hands on him. One after the next his fists pummeled my face. I could hear my jawbone knock into my skull. The longer the fight carried on the quicker Edwin seemed to get. And the slower I became. But I kept stalking him down, trying to get off a shot or two. With my face smashed up and covered in blood, Pat jumped in and tried to separate Edwin and me. After a struggle, Edwin backed off. He danced around, taunting me. He picked up his coat and walked away. "Yo, you got heart," Pat said.

I wiped the blood from my face but it kept pouring out of my nose. My eye swelled shut. My head throbbed. My ego hurt. Pat and I walked block after block with no direction. "How could I get beat down like this?" I kept asking. I went to my mom's house and sat on the stoop, hiding my wounds behind a pair of sunglasses. I didn't want her or my dad to see me banged up. I knew she would put the blame on me, like she did in the past. As a devout Catholic, my mom felt any punishment I received came from the sins I committed. And I couldn't go to my father. He didn't let anything get between him and his numbers. And if I did manage to steal his attention, would he care?

The next day I found out Edwin broke my nose and fractured my orbital bone. But the fractured orbital and the broken nose didn't worry me. Because I knew those wounds would heal. My lack of competence worried me. Before that fight I thought I was tough. I held my own on the streets. I had five years of Tae Kwon Do training. But Edwin came along and challenged my self-belief. For weeks the fight ate me up inside. I tried to come up with reasons why I got beat down. I told myself Edwin was tougher because he spent time in Rikers. I thought maybe I had an off day. But I narrowed my loss down to incompetence.

Over the next few weeks I became obsessed with transforming myself into a better street fighter. I scoured every martial arts magazine I could get my hands on, breezing past the fluff about Tae Kwon Do. There has to be something practical, I kept telling myself. I needed an answer. And then, on the page staring back at me was Frank Cucci, the Navy Seal and hand-to-hand combat expert. Navy Seals are badass, I thought. And Frank Cucci sounded like a badass name. I read the advertisement until I could remember every word. He told me how I could turn my body into a weapon and defense mechanism. It was what I needed to hear at the time.

When the Frank Cucci VHS tapes showed up at my mom's house I devoured them. I studied the Navy Seal as he showed each technique. He walked me through Kali and Filipino wrestling, Jiu Jitsu and boxing. But I knew about those martial arts. I needed something different. Then Cucci's assistant strapped a set of pads around his forearms. And Frank Cucci displayed something I never saw before. He smashed the pads with kicks and punches. He pierced them with his knees and his elbows. He did everything with power and technique. It wasn't flashy. It was simple. It was practical. And it was what I needed to be a better street fighter. He called the martial art, Thai boxing.

I went to a martial arts supply store in New York City and bought a pair of pads like the ones I saw in the video. I recruited my brother, Andrew. We moved the furniture in my mom's living room to give us ample space. And we went to work. Day after day we wrecked shop. I had no idea what I was doing. I mimicked Frank Cucci as best as I could. The kicks, the knees, the elbows, and the punches, I loved the force I had to put into hitting pads. But my mom didn't like it. For one, we were destroying the house. And two, she didn't want us fighting. She thought fighting was for people in poverty. And growing up in one of the most impoverished areas of the Philippines, she didn't want her family doing anything to bring us back to that level.

My mom kicked my brother and me out of the living room and we moved our training space to the garage. Inside the garage I hung a canvas bag and for hours a day I pounded the bag until my knuckles bled out. I waited a few days for them to heal. And I went at it again. Years later my mom had to get her garage fixed because the wooden frame leaned to one side. I like to think the damage was from the abuse the old structure took from me beating on the bag.

The garage, though, became more than a training space. The

garage became my thinking place, the place where I reflected on the direction of my life. Did I hit the bag to become a better street fighter? Did I want to throw my life away for the streets? My self-respect and need for street respect were at war for too long. And the truth is, I grew tired of pretending. I grew tired of silencing the voice telling me to rise up. At twenty years old I had no direction. I knew I had to change the course of my life or wind up dead or in jail. But then there was Edwin? I knew I could run into guys like him at anytime.

CHAPTER TWO
TOMMY THAI

"A teacher is never a giver of Truth; He is a guide, a pointer to the Truth."
- Bruce Lee

In 1996 I outgrew my mom's garage. But I needed to keep training. I swore to myself after the street fight with Edwin I'd never find myself in the same predicament. Not that I was looking for fights. But I wanted the ability to throw down with anyone, anywhere, at anytime. And I needed a practical martial art to help me. Thai boxing was that martial art. But to improve, I had to find a trainer. In the late '90s, though, finding a Thai boxing gym was difficult.

The UFC was going through the dark ages. Aside from boxing gyms, fighter's gyms were few and far between. Coaches like Phil Nurse and Steve Milles and Simon Burgess were coming up, but they ran Muay Thai programs in health clubs around New York City. Coming from the streets, I didn't feel comfortable walking into those places. I thought people would judge me or I might find myself surrounded by people who didn't understand where I was coming from. So I continued to pound away on the canvas bag in my mom's garage.

One day I was walking through the Bowery and passed a storefront on Fifth Street. I saw something hanging in the back of the store. The silhouette looked like the punching bag I hung in my mom's garage, except longer. I kept walking but my curiosity bubbled. I stopped, turned around, and walked back to have another peek in the window. I took a closer look and saw four ring posts attached to the floor. And ring ropes that hung down from post to post like someone was in the middle of pulling them tighter. I looked up at the sign outside: TRISTAR FITNESS.

I looked at the gym from the outside wondering whether or not I should go in. I never entered a fighter's gym before. "Keep walking and come back another day," I told myself. But I paused and thought about what I wanted. I thought about the Edwin fight and how he nearly beat me to death. If I wanted to handle myself on the streets, I had to go in. And I had to go in now.

I stepped inside and a man tinkering with the ring came up to me. "I'm Wayne," he said.

"What do you guys do here?" I asked.

"Muay Thai."

I knew about Thai boxing from the Frank Cucci videos. "You mean with elbows and kicks and knees and stuff?"

"Yeah, same thing. I have a Thai trainer comin' in and we're gonna start classes on..."

"I'll be there," I said.

We called him Tommy Thai. But his real name was Sitsutam Watacharantakul. Tommy was in his late thirties. He was a retired Muay Thai fighter from Southern Thailand with eighty fights to his name. Looking at him you would've never guessed he was an ex-fighter. For a Thai boxer, I always thought his hands and feet were small—until he started using them on me. And he didn't have an aggressive nature. He smiled a lot. And he had a belly, the result of his love for food. Aside from teaching Muay Thai, Tommy opened Thai restaurants around the East coast. But behind his non-threatening stature he was a solid dude.

I started training at Tristar with guys like me. Each of us came from the streets. Each of us came from broken homes. And each of us, in some way or another, had absentee fathers. So we understood each other. We also understood we'd have the advantage if we had to throw down on the streets, because we were the fighters with a real Thai fighter training us.

I learned most of the fundamentals with those guys and Tommy. Tommy taught us when to go hard and when to slow down. Sometimes we strapped on giant boxing gloves and banged out, trying to take each other's heads off. Other times we sparred with no protection, going as light as we could. Sabai, sabai, Tommy would say—relax, relax. Tommy jumped in the ring now and again and moved around with us too. He peppered us with powerful punches and kicks, smiling and scowling and smiling again. He had an enjoyable way of expressing himself, making the grueling training fun.

During one of our sparring sessions Tommy kept landing

his low kick on my thigh. He could tell my frustration was growing and I didn't know what to do. "Bong, bong," he said—block, block. But when I blocked we clashed shins and I felt a jolt of pain run through my lower leg, as if Tommy struck me with a pipe. Getting used to the pain took a few months. And I say "getting used to the pain" because the hurt never went away. I just became more effective at hiding it.

My sparring sessions with Tommy proved to me he walked the walk. And coming from the streets I respected that. I didn't want someone teaching me from the sidelines, standing around with his arms crossed barking orders. I was tested. And I wanted a coach who was tested just the same.

The more time I spent with Tommy the closer we became. And the strange Thai guy with a thick accent became my first coach. Between rounds he made sure I had my water. He massaged my muscles. He stretched me out. He taught me how to take care of my body. But Tommy taught me more than what he knew about the sport of Muay Thai. Tommy introduced me to the traditions of Muay Thai as well. He taught me about the mongkon, the headpiece worn by fighters as they entered the ring, and how each gym had their own custom mongkon. He taught me about the prajiads, the armbands worn by fighters throughout the fight. They held deep meaning to fighters, he said. The armbands were made from scraps of cloth that came from the fighter's mom or dad. And sometimes, the armband would have a lock of hair or other personal artifact woven into the braid. Tommy also showed me how to do the wai kru, the customary dance performed before each fight.

Outside of the gym Tommy taught me other aspects of Thai culture too. He cooked me tom yung, a Thai soup made with lime leaves and lemongrass and other Thai spices. Tommy's kindness meant something to me because no older male ever taught me anything or gave me anything. Not even my own father, even when the attempt fell on my behalf.

When I was younger my father studied Tae Kwon Do at S. Henry Cho's on the Upper East Side. I thought it would be a great idea to follow him along one day, to get to see him outside of the house and do some father and son bonding. So he grabbed his gym bag and we headed to the dojo. When we got there I was filled with excitement. We walked up the stairs and I smelled muscle liniment wafting in the air. I didn't know it at the time, but the smell would grow so familiar throughout my Muay Thai career that I often joked around about using it as cologne. When we entered the dojo I saw these guys in karate gis. The same gi I saw hanging out of my father's gym bag at home.

"Hana. Tul. Set. Net," the instructor called out numbers in Korean and the guys in gis yelled them back.

When my father took the floor he shocked me. He barely spoke at home. He wasn't animated. But at the dojo he expressed himself through his art. He was competent and poised. And for once, I looked up to my father. I asked my mom if I could join the gym because my father, surprisingly enough, inspired me. And she gave me the okay. But after I started training at my father's dojo, my father and I grew further apart. And then my dad stopped showing up at the gym.

To this day I don't know why. I wonder if I infringed on something that belonged to him. Maybe I overstepped my boundaries, because my father continued to bring me to class. But he never went in. And he never showed interest in TKD again.

Three months after I started training with Tommy he walked into the gym and asked me if I wanted to fight. I lit up inside. I couldn't believe I'd have the chance to scrap and not get in trouble. I didn't ask who my opponent was. I didn't ask what weight I was fighting at. I just said yes. After all, I fought on the streets since I was younger. How different could fighting in the ring be?

Before the days of YouTube, researching my opponents was hard. But we managed to get our hands on a VHS tape of one of my opponent's Vale Tudo fights. I noticed how crisp his hand skills were. I had some experience throwing my hands, but he was good. We found out he fought in the Golden Gloves. And if that wasn't enough, he fought guys who went on to fight in the UFC. I realized this wasn't going to be anything like a street fight. And for the first time since entering the gym, I felt afraid. But at the same time this was everything I wanted.

As my coach, Tommy was doing a great job of transforming my body to withstand the fight. But it was my mind he gripped like a vice. Tommy sat me down and we talked about the fight. We talked about ring strategy and how to avoid and negate strong punchers. We drilled a lot of clinch techniques. He taught me how to stay on the outside and score with kicks. And he taught me how to close the distance and dig my knees into my opponent's body and thighs. This was the first time I was training with intention, not only to become a better street fighter, but also to fight and win. I soaked up everything he taught me.

The fight venue was in Staten Island at a boxing gym that seated fifty or sixty people. Tommy and I entered the venue and people were showing Tommy lots of respect. Tommy intrigued people because he was the real deal. Having him, the Thai, in my corner felt good. I felt confident but also scared. There's something different between fighting in the ring and fighting on the streets. On the streets, a fight breaks out in an instant. You don't have time to think about who your opponent is or what he might do. There's no game plan. You act and react. Make adjustments on the spot. And hope for the best.

But with sport fighting you know who your opponent is long before the first bell rings. You prepare for weeks and months in advance. You get to see them on tape. You have time to think about the fight and possible outcomes. You think about the audience. The venue. And you remember as you are preparing for them, they are preparing for you.

My opponent and I stood across the ring from each other and I could see his confidence radiating. But I knew I wanted this. I knew I belonged there. I told myself he was just a man who had fights. But so did I. Maybe not in the ring. But I had them. And he was going to have to kill me to stop me, because even if I didn't yet have the skills, I had the heart. "Don't punch. Clinch and kick," I reminded myself before the first bell rang.

When we met in the middle of the ring for the first round my opponent came out as expected, with heavy hands. I tried to exchange with him, throwing jabs and low kicks, but I wasn't finding any success. I weathered his barrage of punches and escaped the first round.

"Clinch! Work his thighs and body with your knees!" Tommy said as I sat on the stool trying to regain my composure. Then the bell rang. I went out for the second round wanting to make Tommy happy by doing what he told me. But I couldn't find a way past my opponent's hands. I tried a kick-punch combo Tommy and I had worked on during training. I kicked my opponent's body. And when he tried to cover I fired a straight right punch at his head and landed. I couldn't believe the technique worked. So I kicked and then punched him again. It landed. He was on his back foot and slowed down. His hands weren't a threat anymore. I closed the distance and clinched. The crowd roared and I dug the points of my knees into my opponent's thighs and body. Between the second and third round my opponent couldn't come out for the bell.

When the referee raised my hand the joy of winning overcame me. It was a feeling I'd go on to chase the rest of my fight career. I felt proud of myself for dominating a fighter with more experience than me. And putting my skills to use in a real way felt great. I wanted to celebrate. But Tommy kept me in check. He reminded me not to get too cocky or showboat. He taught me how to stay classy in victory.

We went to the back room and I turned to Tommy and I noticed he had tears in his eyes. I didn't know how to react. The only person I ever made cry was my mom. And hers were tears of grief. I wish her and my father were there to see me in a different light. But I had to keep my fighting a secret because my mom would never approve. She would've thought making a living as a fighter would be impossible.

"You. Mr. Classic," Tommy said. I wasn't sure what he meant. The nickname could've meant anything. But words are powerful. When someone like Tommy gives you a nickname, you want to live up to the title. I wanted to be whatever Mr. Classic meant. But because I didn't know what the name meant, I had to carve out a meaning of my own. I carried Mr. Classic with pride, and from that moment on everything I did represented who I thought Mr. Classic should be.

The following months Tommy and I grew even closer. He

was no longer my coach. He was a friend. He was a mentor. He was, in a strange way, becoming the father I never had. So when I heard the news that Tommy was going back to Thailand my world changed. I was loyal to Tommy. But I never opened up to him about my past troubles with fighting and running the streets. I never told Tommy about my absentee father or how Tommy became like a father to me. I didn't want to pressure Tommy into sticking around. I knew he had other plans for his life.

Not too long after Tommy left, Tristar Fitness fell apart. Wayne owed money to people and had to close down the gym. But I felt blessed I had Tommy as my first coach. He taught me valuable lessons about life and fighting. He taught me about respect and tradition. He showed me I didn't have to fight out of anger. And for an anger-filled street kid like me, that was important. But more importantly, he taught me to go after my desires in life, not for fortune or fame, but with love and passion. Tommy was the epitome of what I think Muay Thai should be. And I am in great debt to him for who I am today. He gave me a part of his culture. And his culture became a part of who I am.

CHAPTER THREE
FROM SON TO FATHER

"Never be afraid to fall apart because it is an opportunity to rebuild yourself the way you wish you had been all along."
- Rae Smith

My entire world existed on Two Hundred and Eighth Street in The Ville. I grew up there, made most of my closest friends there, and met my first love, Mildred, there. Mildred was the older sister of my brother, Andrew's, best friend. And although she came from a broken home she was different from the other girls in the neighborhood. Mildred was hard working and responsible. She took care of her sick mother, helped raise her younger brother and sister. And in her senior year of high school she put herself into a work and study program.

I met Mildred at a pivotal time in my life. I was nineteen years old and growing tired of doing non-productive things on the streets day in and day out. She was one of the few positive people I knew. And that attracted me, because I wanted more from life. So I spent more time with her and less time with my friends. And when Mildred got her own apartment, I stayed with her once in a while to get away from my mom and dad. We began seeing more of each other, and although Mildred and I never talked about marriage, we knew we wanted to be together.

In 1998 we had our son, Jube. From that moment life took on a new meaning. I knew the instant Jube came into my life I had to get myself together. I wanted to be the father I never had. My son would need me to guide and love him and show him how to be a man. But at the time I was still learning how to become a man of my own. Since my father never taught me what that meant, I didn't know how I'd teach Jube those things. But I knew I'd fight like hell to figure it out.

My dad had a hands-off approach to raising his sons. He often hid in the basement of our house or sat at the kitchen table writing lottery numbers. I wanted to be more hands-on, because I knew so intimately the psychological and emotional effects of neglect. So I made a pact to myself that no matter how hard fatherhood became, I'd be there for Jube. I was a father. His father. And I wore the duty with pride.

At that time I was working for Nature Food Centers. But I needed a job that paid more and provided my family with benefits. I starting applying for jobs and I landed a position as a delivery driver for FedEx. From the day I started working at the company they gassed my head up. They told me if I did a good job I could climb the corporate ranks and become a manager. But I didn't want to hear any of the hype. I was there for one reason, to provide for my family. Working at FedEx wasn't something I planned to do with my life. And the day-in, day-out grind made me miserable. But I swallowed my pride and showed up to work everyday.

Right around the same time I was hired as a delivery driver, Mildred and I bought a house on Two Hundred and Twelfth Place and Hillside Avenue in The Ville. The old house needed a lot of repairs. The roof leaked. The water pipes leaked. Appliances broke down or needed to be replaced. And we didn't have money to hire repairmen. So I taught myself how to be a handyman. On one hand, learning new skills and being the man of the house felt good. But at the same time I couldn't keep up with everything. And the stress of owning a home began to eat away at my life.

My idea of fatherhood and family life was also different from the reality facing me. When I wasn't working at FedEx, I was working on the house. I couldn't spend a lot of time with Jube. Mildred and I stressed over the bills. And we both avoided talking about anything that would lead to confrontation. But we stuck the relationship out, thinking better days would come once everything was in order. As life dragged on, though, the idea of order faded.

Before we had Jube, Mildred's mom passed away from kidney failure. Being the oldest of three, Mildred took on the responsibility of raising her brother and sister. Without Mildred, they'd be on the streets. So when we bought the house we let Mildred's brother and sister live with us. Although taking them in was the right thing to do, it wasn't the most ideal living condition.

Mildred's sister, Jennifer, wasn't much trouble to have around. But her brother, Roland, came from the streets. He reminded me of myself before Jube was born. Most times, he hung around the house and smoked weed with his friends. And he didn't respect our rules. But unlike me, Roland was content with that lifestyle. I was trying to move away from the streets. I didn't want the stuff around Jube. And to top it off, the house was a mess. Since I worked a lot, keeping the place in order fell on Mildred and her brother and sister. But they never pitched in to help. And the fridge was empty. I was working my tail off to support everyone and it felt like no one gave a damn.

As life at home diminished, Mildred and I grew further apart. To see less of each other she worked days and I took the night shift at FedEx. When I was home I hung out in the basement to avoid everyone. After Jube was born I distanced myself from drinking. But one night I picked up the bottle again. And I began drowning my anger in alcohol. If I didn't pass out, I blacked out. I broke things around the house. I blamed everyone around me for the negativity in my life.

I could accept my responsibilities as a father. But I couldn't accept responsibility for Mildred's lack of desire to improve and her brother and sister's inability to contribute. And the house, the one thing that should've brought us closer together, pulled us apart. My anger grew.

I remember going to a party one night to escape everything at home. But I became more uncomfortable as the night went on. I was drinking heavily, and without a concern, jumped into my '94 Ford Contour and drove home. When I neared the entrance ramp of the Jackie Robinson Parkway I floored the car, hitting eighty miles an hour around the bend. The car went spinning out of control. When the Contour came to a stop in the middle of the ramp, by pure luck, I didn't hit anything or anyone. But my reckless behavior didn't end there.

Another afternoon I was hanging out in the neighborhood with Mildred and Jube. We had an argument over something small. Instead of letting the argument go, my ego got the best of me. My emotions rose. I had this anger pinned up inside for so long and I had nowhere to direct my fury. As Mildred and I yelled at each other my fuse grew shorter. And I exploded. With Jube in the stroller, I ran. I ran into the street without a care in the world. Cars whizzed by. Jube's body bounced up and down in the stroller. I heard Mildred yelling behind me. But I kept going. I wanted to escape.

I did a lot of regretful things during that time of my life, to myself and to other people. But putting my son's life in jeopardy haunted me. And I broke down. Life had become too much for me to handle. I tried so hard for so long to do the right thing, the family thing. I didn't want to be like my mom, who was angry at the world. And I didn't want to be like my dad, who cut himself off from his family. But in truth, I had become like both of them.

Mildred and I decided to give our relationship one last shot. Since most of our stress came from the house and not having free time and extra money, we sold it and moved into an apartment on Francis Lewis Boulevard. Life seemed okay for a while but our problems returned. Mildred's brother and sister followed us to the apartment. And on more than one occasion I had to throw Roland out for smoking weed. And Mildred and I resented each other more and more. We were at each other's throats all the time. And I still had deep-seated anger issues that rose to the surface.

But I kept thinking about Jube. He was young but the stress had to be affecting him. He was living in the middle of madness. And I didn't want him growing up in a stressful environment. I had to ask myself if I wanted to keep living in turmoil. I had this feeling deep down in the core of my being that a better life awaited me. Tommy Thai gave me a glimpse of what was possible if I applied myself. But everything I learned under Tommy I put to the wayside. The focus. The determination. The discipline. I lost everything. And I reverted back to the person I was before I stepped into Tristar Fitness. I was angry at myself because I knew I could do better.

But I was at a loss. I had no clear path in front of me. And in life, if there's no clear path in front of you, you have to take out the machete and make one. I began thinking about where I wanted to be in life. And I thought about who or what was in the way of me getting there. And I started clearing a path.

I knew my relationship with Mildred wasn't going anywhere. We met when I was still running around on the streets. But after the birth of Jube my mindset shifted. I wanted to grow and improve. And Mildred was content with her life. I had to ask myself if the relationship was worth sticking out. If I did, I'd be closer to Jube, but I risked being unhappy and my unhappiness would turn me into my father. If I left, I'd be further away from Jube. But I'd be happier. My relationship with Jube would be better. I sat and thought about the possible scenarios. Which decisions made sense? Which didn't?

Later on in life I learned as a fighter that timing is everything. If your timing is off you're going to have a tough fight ahead of you. Life works the same way. I understood Mildred and her brother and sister lost their mom and, in a sense, they themselves were lost. But I was no better than they were. I came from a broken home too. I was struggling to find myself as a man, never mind a father. It was bad timing for all of us.

I decided to leave Mildred. Everything was so bad between us for so long I didn't expect her to hold on. But there was no emotion. Not a word. Making the decision was tough because I'd be away from Jube. I knew in the long run my relationship with Jube would strengthen. But to be a better father, I had to figure out how to be a better man first.

With nowhere to go, I moved back into my mom's house, where I slept in the basement. I tried to keep myself together for my son. But somewhere along the way I took a turn for the worse. My job at FedEx fell apart soon after. My supervisor warned me on two occasions not to drive with the doors open or with my seatbelt unbuckled. But I didn't care. I lost my house. My family. My son. My pride. Losing my job wouldn't have taken anything else from me. When I was caught for the third time and they fired me, part of me was happy.

I still had Jube to worry about though. So I took on medial jobs to make ends meet. I delivered gasoline to gas stations and police departments. I worked as a process server for the city of Queens. Then I was hired at an electric company and had the chance to get into the union. But this nine-to-five thing didn't sit well with me. So I quit.

I needed a career that would give me control over my life, a career that would let me make my own hours and be my own boss. And I needed a career that would give me the time and money I needed to raise Jube. Once again I thought back to my time with Tommy Thai. Training under him was one of the few times I did something positive with my life. So I began formulating a plan to get myself out of the basement and back to the gym.

ROUND TWO: FINDING MY RYTHYM

CHAPTER FOUR
WINNING ISN'T EVERYTHING

*"It takes a little courage, and a little self control. And some grim
determination, if you want to reach the goal. It takes a great deal of
striving, and a firm and stern set chin. No matter what the battle, if you
really want to win, there's no easy path to glory. There's no road to fame.
Life however we may view it, is no simple parlor game - but it's prizes
call for fighting, for endurance and for grit. For a rugged disposition that
will not quit."*
- Navy Seal Master Chief

On our office wall at CROM Physical Culture, above my desk, hangs a plaque—a gift I received in December of 2004 from Mildred and Jube. The plaque is made of wood with gold trim running along the inside border. Scratches and nicks have dulled the plaque's glossy finish. But the printed text is still legible. The title reads *OUTSTANDING ACHIEVEMENTS AWARD*. And below my name, printed in much finer text is *For your six week love and dedication of MUAY THAI*. Underneath that, *"all it takes is heart."*

Mildred and Jube gave me the plaque when I returned home from my first trip to Thailand to compete at the International Federation of Muaythai Amateurs annual tournament. Despite parting ways with Mildred I've kept the plaque as a reminder to keep hunting down my goals. And although my goals have changed over the course of my life, my main goal back in 2004 was to fight the best fighters in the world and see if a professional fighting career was in my future. But to fight the best in the world I had to get out of New York City. And I needed a coach to help me get there.

I ran Metropolis Muay Thai, my first martial arts program, out of Church Street Boxing Gym, deep in the sub-basement of Twenty-Five Park Place. I hung handmade flyers around the city to bring in members. And I managed to get a few people to train during lunchtime. One day this guy walked in I never saw before. By the looks of him, I could tell he wasn't from the area.

"Can I take the class?" he asked.

"Yeah, man. You're welcome to join us," I said.

As I taught class I noticed this guy had skills. So I kept my eye on him, trying to figure out who he was and where he was from.

"You wanna kick-spar?" he asked after class.

"Sure, let's go for it."

Right from the get-go this guy gave me problems. His technique was sound. He used his hands well. He was smart with his defense. I could tell he could've kicked my ass but was holding back.

"Where you from? What's your name?"

"Milwaukee. Jason," he said. And he went on to tell me about his training under Duke Rufus and Kongnapa. And how he was on vacation and wanted to get a training session in before he went home. Then he told me about his plans to move to New York City.

"Look me up," I said. "If you move out here we should train together."

Within a year Jason Strout moved to New York City. Training under him was like nothing I ever experienced before. The only coach I had before him was Tommy Thai. And Jason was the complete opposite. I thought us folk from New York City talked fast. But here was this guy from Milwaukee who, when he spoke, I could barely make out what he was saying. And compared to Tommy Thai, Jason had a hard-nosed style of training me. He'd smack me in the face between rounds. He'd yell and curse at me on top of his lungs from the corner. But despite his unorthodox coaching style, I admired Jason. His passion for the fight game was contagious. He was one of the few people I knew at the time who loved fighting more than me—apparent by the hundreds of VHS tapes he had of old boxing fights.

Jason was also younger than me. Seeking out a younger trainer wasn't typical for an older fighter, especially since we were equal in experience. But there was something about what he knew. And I wanted to know it too. Even if he didn't teach me things about Thai culture like Tommy, Jason put in the time and effort. And his dedication showed me he cared. And once he figured out I'd listen to him whether he yelled at me or not, or whether he smacked me around or not, our relationship grew.

Under Jason's tutelage, in 2004 I applied to fight on Team USA at the International Federation of Muaythai Amateurs tournament in Bangkok. Fairtex sponsored Team USA, and to become part of the team I had to go through them. I applied to represent the team and they approved my application and I passed the interview. But I felt the process was too easy. I wanted to earn my spot on Team USA. I was—and still am—not one for handouts. I've always believed rewards are the fruit of hard work. So before I left for Thailand I took a fight as a test to see if I could represent Team USA.

Steve Milles and Simon Burgess, the promoters of Mayhem on Mulberry, arranged a fight for me to defend my World Kickboxing Association national belt against Tom Heavey. I knocked Heavey out in the first round in Virginia at the WKA annual tournament in the summer of 2004. But his team claimed I caught him with a lucky hook. So they wanted to fight again. I agreed, never wanting to shy away from anyone, and this time I walked away with the decision win. With the rematch in the bag and another win on my record I felt better about my spot on Team USA. But leaving for Thailand was more difficult than I expected.

At the time, Jube was six years old and although I didn't live with him and Mildred, going to Thailand would be the first time I was away from him for that long—six weeks to be exact. Social media wasn't big yet so I couldn't log onto a computer or look at my phone and see what he was up to, and he couldn't do the same with me. I'd be able to stay in touch with them only through a calling card. I felt bad leaving him for six weeks, but at the same time I wanted to show my son the importance of following his dreams.

I left New York City and headed for Thailand a month earlier than the rest of Team USA. I wanted to get in as much training as I could and show the Thais I meant business. When I arrived, I began to experience with my senses what I saw through video or heard from Tommy Thai. And having left America on only one other occasion, culture shock hit me. I took in the street dogs and the street food, the motorcycles carrying entire families whizzing by, and the laid back ways of Thai people. They never seemed to get excited or show aggression. And since I was non-confrontational by nature, I felt like I fit right in.

Growing up watching my favorite Muay Thai fighters display tenacity in the ring, I thought every gym in Thailand was hardcore, that each fighter was struggling for survival in a rundown camp somewhere in rural Thailand. But Fairtex gym changed my opinions. The gym was immaculate. Training mats covered the floor. And there were four rings, enough for every fighter to train in at the same time. There was a swimming pool, a cafe, and dorms with a choice of air conditioning or electric fans. Because part of me wanted to experience a rougher setting, I opted for a room with an electric fan. I needed some discomfort to keep myself hungry for the battle ahead. But I learned just because Fairtex didn't look hardcore, didn't mean the training was going to be easy.

Six days a week I woke up at dawn and ran. I started out on the street. I made my way over a bridge and past the gym owner's house, where koi fish in a small pond swam in circles. And from there, into the farmlands, where I passed the time thinking of how much I'd love to live in Thailand. Each morning I enjoyed the quiet contemplation of rural life. Houses and buildings and the bustling noise of the city surrounded me for most of my life. And for a city kid like me rural Thailand was refreshing, cleansing in a way to run through the open land and greenery.

I trained twice a day, once in the mornings after my run, and once in the late afternoons after my nap. Each session lasted three or four hours. On pads I worked with a trainer named Jakrit. Jakrit wasn't your average trainer. The finer intricacies of Muay Thai techniques didn't appeal to Jakrit. His sole purpose was to be the constant reminder you were training to fight. And he made sure you didn't forget. When I punched or kicked, Jakrit countered. When my defense was sloppy, he tripped me. When my offense was weak, he taunted me. And after four weeks of training with Jakrit there was nothing any of my opponents could do or say that would've fazed me.

I like to think I impressed Jakrit and the other Thais at Fairtex too. Not because I survived his offensive onslaught everyday—the Thais expected us foreigner fighters to train hard—, but because I busted my hump everyday in training, even with an injury. Before I went to Thailand I injured my right leg. But I wanted to show Fairtex how game I was. So I worked around the injury. Word spread to Mr. Wong, the owner of Fairtex, that I was putting in the rounds and grinding out each training session. And he started to show up to my training sessions. Mr. Wong rarely came out to watch westerners hit pads. So this surprised the other westerners. And impressing the Thais made me feel good.

Saying I didn't learn anything at Fairtex wouldn't be fair. If pad work was the part of training where Jakrit pushed me to my limits, then sparring and clinching was where I slowed down and absorbed as much as I could. I trained with fighters like Kaew and Pepsi—Kaew weighing half of what I weighed but packing two times the power; and Pepsi grinding me down during clinching with his unusually tall stature for a Thai. I also trained with top guys from England, like Steve Wakeling, who already established himself as a top middleweight fighter. There was also Apidej Sit Hirun, a master instructor, known as one of the most lethal left kickers in the game. Each fighter and trainer offered up his time and knowledge, and because of their expertise my confidence soared going into the IFMAs.

Austria is the only place I traveled to before Thailand. I was there for a wedding—a cousin of a cousin. And in my first fight of the tournament I was to face Austria's top amateur fighter, on my thirtieth birthday. A win and advancement to the next bracket, I thought, would be a great gift to myself for the hard work. Mr. Wong, who was curious about me since I arrived at Fairtex, came out to watch my fight against the Austrian. I felt confident in each round that I was winning the fight. And after four rounds the judges awarded me the decision win.

I was proud to advance to the semifinals. I was proud to represent Team USA and Fairtex in a good light. And I thought I made Jakrit and Mr. Wong proud as well. But when I stepped out of the ring Mr. Wong approached me with a look of contempt.

"You could've knocked him out," he said. "I told you—kick harder! You don't have killer instinct." Mr. Wong put me back by his comments because ever since my first fight I entered the ring with a fight-to-the-death mindset. I took his words for what they were—words. There was no way to convince Mr. Wong otherwise. And besides, I was happy he drove from his business in Bangphli to Bangkok to watch me fight, even if he did scold me.

I had a few days off before the semifinals of the IFMAs, where I faced a fighter from Belgium. I stood at five foot nine inches. He was six foot five inches tall. He had a slim build and long limbs. And as soon as the first bell rang the Belgian acquainted me with each of those limbs. In the clinch, he drove his knees into my chin. The referee gave me a standing eight count. But I was far from out of the fight. When I went back to my corner in between rounds Jakrit looked at his arm and began tapping his elbow. Although we couldn't communicate with words, I knew what he wanted me to do. The bell rang and I ground my way through the Belgian's guard, taking a few shots to get close enough to work my elbows into his face.

We battled back and forth for four rounds. And in the end the judges gave the fight to the Belgian. But the scrap was the most exciting fight I've had in my career. Getting the chance to fight to the sounds of live traditional Thai music, to the roars of my teammates, and to the chants of the crowd. The experience was hard to top. And it happened in the birthplace of Muay Thai. But it was also the bloodiest battle I've had. Even though I wore gear from head to toe, the Belgian fighter cut my chin in two places. As I lay there getting stitched up, Jakrit's son stood over me, looking on. Coaches and fighters from other countries came over to say how impressed they were. The experience was a far cry from fighting in New York City. And although I lost to the Belgian, I was proud of myself for following my dreams.

After the fight, to everyone's surprise, news spread that the Belgian fighter wasn't who he said he was. The manager of Team USA went to investigate and found out he fought in the A-Class tournament—the professionals—and lost a few days earlier. The Belgian decided to disguise his record and enter the B-Class tournament—the amateurs—under a new name. When the IFMA officials questioned the Belgian fighter he admitted to everything. His reason? He wanted to fight. And so did I. But I wasn't going to make a fuss over the whole thing. I was never one to complain and I was fine with taking the hand dealt to me. But our team manager persisted and the IFMA officials stripped the Belgian fighter of the bronze medal and gave the award to me instead.

It bothered me the Belgian lied. And I didn't want to accept the bronze in that fashion either. But after a while I accepted the award. After all, I wasn't the fighter who cheated. And I wasn't the person upset after discovering what the Belgian fighter did. I wanted to test myself against the best fighters in the world and see if I was ready to turn pro. So the bronze medal took on new meaning. The Belgian, with twenty-seven pro fights to his name, gave me what I wanted.

CHAPTER FIVE
A FATHER'S ATONEMENT

"Being vulnerable is the only way to allow your heart to feel true pleasure."
- Bob Marley

I worked the floor at New York Sports Club on Madison Avenue, helping clients with their exercises, maintaining the workout area, and picking up whatever privates I could. I was following my dream of becoming a personal trainer, but I wanted to break out and make a name for myself. My past, though, still haunted me. On one hand I felt accomplished with my amateur-fighting career, but on the other hand I still carried with me anger like an anchor in my heart. I blamed my father for a lot of the wrongs in my life. I couldn't open up to my mother. And I wanted to be a better father to Jube. If there was a way to get my thoughts and actions aligned, I knew I'd be more successful in life. That's when I found the Landmark Self-Development Course.

The course promised to break down the wall between where I was and where I wanted to be. The course promised to rid me of the negativity holding me back. The course sounded like everything I needed. But the price tag was six hundred and ninety-five dollars. At the time I was making ten dollars an hour plus commission. Six hundred and ninety-five dollars was a lot of money to invest in a program. I had to cover my costs at home and give money to Mildred for Jube. But I knew in order to grow in business and in life I had to invest in myself too. I wanted to create a future that gave me more time with Jube. I wanted to build a bridge between my father and me. And I wanted to hold myself accountable for my life. I didn't want to point the blame at everyone else for the wrongs in my life. After much consideration, I enrolled.

The course was four days long, with the first three days consisting of exercises to find out what was holding me back. Because there were a lot of people, we broke into small groups. In those groups each of us had to talk about the people or experiences impacting us most. After sharing my experiences with my group, they reinforced what I already knew. They told me I blamed my father for most of the negativity in my life. And they told me that to free myself from this negativity, I had to first free my father.

Members of my group suggested I write a letter to my dad, but I shouldn't let him read what I wrote. Instead, I should use the letter as a way to organize my thoughts and feelings. So I sat down and put the pen to paper and pulled everything out. In the letter I told my father I wished he had spent more time with his sons. I told him how angry I was at him for not being there for my mom. And I told him how disappointed I was at him for not doing anything with his life aside from gambling. I felt freer getting these thoughts and feelings out of my head and onto paper. But this was only the first step.

The next step of the Landmark Course was telling my father face-to-face what I wrote in the letter. To do this, I had to invite my father to the Landmark Course. This, in itself, was a feat because my father barely spoke in person. Getting him on the phone to invite him to the event would be even more difficult. When I called him, I didn't tell him what my invitation was about. But he agreed to show up anyway.

The last day of the Landmark Course I sat in the crowd and wondered if my father would come. He hated social gatherings and avoided them at all costs. My brothers were there. My mom was there. Then, to my surprise, my father showed up. I still didn't tell him what was going to happen though. My family and I sat in the crowd waiting for my turn. I watched the other speakers before me. They looked educated and competent. Doubt rushed into my head. I heard the voice from the stage. "Ladies and gentlemen, please welcome, Chris Romulo." I stood up, walked up to the stage, and took the microphone.

"Dad," I said. "I want to let you know I'm sorry—I'm sorry for using you as an excuse on why I can't accomplish anything of value in my life. I want you to know it's not your fault. And from this moment on I take full responsibility for my life." For ten minutes I stood in front of two hundred and fifty strangers and told my father how I felt about our relationship. It wasn't the first time I cried, but it was the first time I cried in public. I resented my father for so long, that when I opened up to him from stage, I felt free—free from the pain, the blame, and the shame I carried for almost thirty years.

When I came down from the stage my brothers embraced me. My mother cried and told me she loved me and she was proud of me. They were happy I put the past behind me and showed my father, for the first time in a long time, some love. But when I turned to my father, a simple "Thank you" and "I understand" was all he said. But whether or not he was thankful, whether or not he understood, I'll never know. Nothing changed between the two of us. He stayed in his shell, untouchable and unapproachable.

Despite feeling like my speech fell on my father's deaf ears, getting up on stage helped me cross a major threshold in my life. Until that moment, public speaking terrified me. I would've rather step into a ring and face the toughest fighter in my weight class than step onto a stage and stand in front of a crowd. But after my Landmark speech, my fear succumbed to the realization that I could use my voice to express myself in a meaningful way. I realized I could also use my voice as a weapon to destroy adversity.

ROUND THREE: SETTLING INTO THE FIGHT

CHAPTER SIX
THE COWBOY AT CHURCH

"Defeat is not a bitter pill unless you swallow it."
- Joe Clark

T he Church of St. Paul the Apostle sat on the corner of Columbus Avenue and West Sixtieth Street in Manhattan. The archaic stone facade contrasted the modern metropolis towering above and around it. On the outside of the building a large mural showed St. Paul meeting the resurrected Jesus on the road to Damascus. And underneath the mural, a set of stairs led to the church basement, where, for close to a decade, I fought and resurrected my own life as a Muay Thai fighter in New York City. But the two hundred-year-old cathedral was more than a place for fighters to exchange blows. It was a place for couples to exchange vows, my mother and father being one of them.

My parents were married in the Church of St. Paul the Apostle in 1973. And for over thirty years they never returned. Never, that is, until 2005, when I had my second-to-last amateur fight. I won the World Kickboxing Association's North American title in 2005 from a game Canadian fighter named Jason Cutbill. I fought in Thailand at the IFMAs. And Jason Strout and I talked about me turning pro. I didn't get into fighting to stay in the amateurs. I wanted to fight the best in the world. But to fight the best, I had to turn pro. First, I needed a few more fights. Justin Blair, the promoter of Friday Night Fights, said he found me "some kick boxer from Colorado."

With the success I was having, I thought inviting my parents down to the church so they could see me in action was a good idea. For a long time, my mother didn't support the path I was taking. She wanted me to go to college and become a doctor or lawyer or find some other white-collar, well-paying job. But I wanted to prove to her I could find success by carving out my own path. I wanted to show my mom and dad how important Muay Thai was for me, and how doing what I loved would take me places. I also thought getting my parents back to the place they were married would be a good idea. In a way, I was hoping my father would wake up and realize he was neglecting my mom and isolating himself from his children.

Long before mixed martial arts fans called him "The Cowboy," I knew Donald Cerrone as an amateur kick boxer, a kick boxer who was coming to New York City to stop the success I was having in the amateur circuit. And that's all I knew. So for the first time in my career I did something I never did before. I didn't research my opponent, and I didn't add anything new to my game. "He's from Colorado," I said. "I'll just make sure my cardio is on point."

When I saw Cerrone at the weigh-ins I realized how tough of a fight I had ahead of me. Cerrone looked big for a middleweight. And when he stepped on the scale he came in over the agreed fight weight, which was one hundred and sixty-five pounds. He couldn't cut the extra weight and Justin Blair asked me if I still wanted to take the fight. I never refused a fight over a few pounds. And besides, Cerrone traveled from Colorado. The least I could do was give him the courtesy of accepting the fight. "Screw it. Let's do this," I said. Looking back, I realize I was trying to rationalize the situation. As I went through my fight career I learned the importance of coming in on weight, if not to make everything easier for me, then as a sign of respect to the other fighter and promoter.

The next night I arrived at the church and settled in for the fight. The referee went over the rules and regulations with the fighters and coaches. We broke out to our respective warm-up rooms. Then, during one of my passes through the venue I noticed Cerrone in the middle of the ring, moving around, shadowboxing, touching the ropes and canvas. I did the same thing before each of my fights. But on this night I didn't do it.

I didn't do another thing that night as well. Before each of my fights I hung out in the warm-up room, relaxing and focusing on the fight ahead. But my ego was too big after winning the WKA national title and fighting in Thailand. So I went out into the crowd and mingled with my family and friends. Jason kept telling me to chill out but I didn't listen. Then, I saw a figure in the corner of my eye, a silhouette of a man sitting on the stage overlooking the ring. It was Cerrone, sitting there, focused, staring out into the ring. I could tell from his demeanor his head was in the fight. His intensity shone from the shadows of where he sat.

Since my days with Tommy Thai I stayed true to the traditions of Muay Thai. I always wore the prajiads and mongkon. But I wanted to do something different for this fight. I wanted to find a way to represent with my Filipino heritage while staying true to the traditions of Muay Thai. So I took the Filipino flag, draped it over my head, and then put the mongkon around my head. When fight time came, I walked toward the door of the warm-up room wearing a mix of Thai and Filipino garb. The door opened and I saw Cerrone standing in the ring. He was wearing a pair of American flag trunks. I stepped out into the venue and the crowd starting chanting "USA! USA! USA!" A group of ironworkers, who Justin Blair invited to the fights, was sitting ringside and when they saw me, stared at me with contempt. I was the hometown guy. I built my name fighting in the basement of the church. New York City was mine. Cerrone was the out-of-towner. But it didn't matter. I might as well have been the Iron Sheik walking out to face Hulk Hogan at Madison Square Garden.

When the fight started I buried the blunder in the back of my head and regained my wits. I kept kicking Cerrone's front thigh like a lumberjack trying to chop down a tree. But he didn't budge. He walked forward, countering with punches. I had a reputation as a fighter who could take punches, but I was also known for not seeing them come in. And Cerrone landed a straight right that I felt in the ends my toes. Cerrone pounced. But by luck, I managed to get out of the round.

I wobbled to my corner and sat on the stool and Jason laid into me. "What the fuck are you doing?" he said. "Keep your hands up." And the second round came as quickly as the first round ended. Cerrone came after me like a man on a mission. He trapped me in the corner and kicked me. He landed another straight right. I dropped. But I popped back up as quickly as I fell. The ref gave me a standing eight count. Experienced fighters, smart fighters, take the time to recover. But I was so fueled with ego I wanted to prove I belonged there. "Are you okay?" the ref said. I nodded my head and put my hands up. Seconds later Cerrone threw another straight right that punctured my guard like a piston. My head hinged backward. A towel soared into the ring. The ref waved his hands. The doctor climbed to the canvas. The fight was over.

Ego is a tricky thing. As a martial artist you spend your life trying to eliminate ego from the human equation. But as a fighter you need to keep a little bit of ego with you. You can't let it control you, though, and trick you into making miscalculated decisions. That night, and the weeks leading up to the fight, satiating my ego was more important than satiating my drive to improve and turn pro. I stepped down from the ring, head hanging low. My family and friends awaited me. "You'll do better next time," they all said.

CHAPTER SEVEN
THE CANADIAN TRILOGY

"We must bring our own light to the darkness."
- Chuck Bukowski

As a coach, I tell my students that confidence may get them into a fight, but competence gets them through it. I learned this mindset when I took on the more experienced Alex Ricci from one of Canada's top Muay Thai gyms, Siam #1. I fought two of his teammates back-to-back, Rick Sanita and Oliver Davis.

I fought Sanita in my fifth professional Muay Thai fight. At the time I was still building my experience and honing my skills. A fight with Sanita, my team thought, would tell us where I stood in the middleweight division. Plus we knew the matchup was good. He spent time in Thailand and being from Siam #1 we expected him to fight with a traditional Thai style. I carried myself the same way in the ring. We'd surely display a technical showing for fight fans.

As expected, Sanita came out technical for the first round of our fight. He kept busy, firing away his kicks. But I evaded and attacked with ease. On one occasion, though, he threw a body kick but I didn't evade. Instead, as his shin touched my ribcage I wrapped my left arm around his leg, pulled his leg up and back, and wrenched his body closer to mine. He hobbled on his back leg, trying to control his balance, which worked out even better. Because his position gave me a chance to fire my right leg to the side of his head.

In training, if your shin hits the pads just right, it sounds like a shotgun blast. When I hit Sanita on the side of his head with my right shin it sounded like that. I watched as he stumbled backward, turned, and dropped onto the canvas. He laid on the ring face down trying to push himself up. He couldn't muster the strength though. The referee counted to eight and asked Sanita if he wanted to continue. Sanita shook his head and the ref waved off the fight. The crowed exploded. I wanted to share in their happiness but I remembered what Tommy Thai taught me—stay humble in victory.

I knocked out fighters before. In fact, I won three of my first four pro fights by knockout. But knocking Sanita out felt different. Sanita came from a reputable gym. He had experience. He was a traditional Thai-style fighter. And he was coming to New York City from Canada to take my crown.

With another knockout on my record I set the precedence that my fights weren't going the distance. Fans knew they'd get their money's worth when I fought. The buzz was strong, and I was becoming the hometown hero in the world of Muay Thai in New York City. But the label extended far beyond the ropes of the ring. Ever since I was younger I wanted to do something better with the Romulo name. I didn't want to carry myself like my father did. Or like his father did. I wanted people to hear "Romulo" and feel inspired. And I wanted to teach my son through example what being a Romulo meant. I felt a duty to stop anyone in his tracks who tried to take my name away from me. So when Siam #1 sent their next killer down, I took the fight without question.

Oliver Davis stood six foot four inches tall. He had the height advantage. He had experience, more experience than Rick Sanita, and more experience than me. I knew his skills would play a factor in the fight, but I was game for the challenge. And besides, the last time I fought someone that tall was at the IFMAs in Thailand, when I faced the Belgian. And he smashed me up. But real fighters take tough fights. If you want to improve as a person you have to face challenges. I looked at fights as puzzles that I had to figure out. Oliver Davis was the next puzzle. And a win over Davis would reconcile my loss to the Belgian fighter at the IFMAs.

Being from Siam #1, we knew Davis would come out like Sanita did, with a traditional Thai style. But because of his height, Jason and I tweaked our game plan. Instead of trying to exchange on the outside, we decided I should evade his long reach and close the distance. From there I could work my knees in the clinch, where I was growing more comfortable as a fighter. I also sparred as many taller training partners as I could to simulate the feeling of standing across from Davis. By the end of training I felt in great condition. I was coming off the knockout win over Sanita. I might've had fear, but I had no doubts that I'd beat Davis.

From the opening bell Davis used his long push kicks to keep me on the outside. I couldn't close the distance or land anything clean. From there, as Jason and I had planned, he followed up with round kicks. But just because you have a game plan, just because you know what your opponent's going to do, doesn't mean anything when he's standing in front of you. There's a big difference between knowing and doing, and during the first round I wasn't doing much. As I buried my frustrations, Davis popped me in the face with a stiff jab and rocked me.

I found my comfort zone in the clinch after three rounds. I stayed as busy as I could, trying to rack up the points I lost in the first two rounds. During one tussle in the clinch, Davis missed my chin with his knee by a hair. He was a lot taller, so I could see how his knee was unintentional. But because knees weren't allowed to the head back then, the referee warned him.

For most of the third and fourth rounds we ground each other down in the clinch, knee for knee. Both of us scored big. In one exchange he threw another high knee, but this time he caught me on the chin. My legs felt like noodles and my knees buckled against each other. I refused to go down. The referee gave Davis another warning. "Take your time," the ref told me. But I was never the type to milk a break. I wanted back in. I shook the pain off and the fight ensued.

"You're losing this fight," Jason said before the fifth round. "You need to do something to stop him." But I didn't know what to do. I don't think either of us knew what to do at the time. I was rather inexperienced and Jason was still building skills as a coach. On the outside Davis was having his way with me. On the inside I was taking damage from his knees. I was confident before the fight. But I was falling apart now. I wasn't showing competence. Without an answer, I jumped off the stool for the fifth and final round. "I gotta stop this guy. There's no way I could let Davis take me out—not in my hometown." I bit down on my mouthpiece, put up my guard, and when the bell rang I marched forward.

Earlier in the fight I found success landing my right cross on Davis' body. So in the final round I went back to the straight right. My eyes locked on his torso and I threw the right cross. Thump. We exchanged hands in a flurry. And we both backed off. Again, I locked my eyes on his torso. I could see him preparing to cover for my body shot. So I faked low and went high. My right cross landed on his chin and he went limp. His upper body tried to find balance above his legs. But his legs took him across the ring. My killer instinct kicked in and I stalked Davis down. I chopped away at his legs with low kicks. I went back to his body. I had him against the ropes. I could hear the sound of the crowd roaring louder and louder with each weapon I landed. I wanted revenge for the last four rounds. I threw a powerful kick against Davis' body that stopped him in his tracks. And then I went for it. I looked up at the giant in front of me and I aimed my kick for Davis' head. My shin smashed against his glove and his glove smashed into the side of his head. He was defenseless. With moments left in the final round the ref stopped the fight.

If I hadn't rallied back in the fifth and final round I would've lost the decision. Even as the hometown fighter. He had me hurt throughout the fight. And I was down on points. That's what I miss about fighting. I miss being the underdog in the fight, the fighter who's hurt but has to dig deep and make a come back in the final moments. I've accomplished a lot in my life. But there's nothing like having your hand raised after coming back from being down on points. And for as much damage as I took in my fight with Davis, I wanted more.

In boxing, Mayweather had wars with Mexican fighters. In mixed martial arts, Sakuraba had wars with the Gracies. And in Muay Thai, I wanted fight fans to know me as the American who stepped up and went to war with Canadian fighters, because Canadians produced great Muay Thai fighters. So when Siam #1 offered us Alex Ricci as my next opponent I jumped at the opportunity. Unlike Sanita and Davis, both good fighters in their own rights, Ricci was more accomplished. He fought in Thailand professionally. I fought there as an amateur. He had fifty professional fights. I had six. Rankings considered him one of the best Canadian fighters in the middleweight division. I was a fighter still coming up through the ranks in the same division. But

I didn't care. I wanted the challenge. I showed the competence to make adjustments in the Davis fight, even if I didn't do so until the end. "We're gonna have this trilogy," was all I thought. "We're gonna take out three Canadians in New York City. This is gonna be huge."

Because Ricci was from the same camp as Sanita and Davis, and since he spent time in Thailand, Jason and I didn't change up our game plan. We expected Ricci to fight like Sanita and Davis, except on a higher level. He had more experience, but we knew the fight would be a slow, technical war. Coming out of the Davis fight I started finding my comfort as a fighter. I liked to sit back the first two rounds and turn the fight up from the third to the fifth round. So that's what we planned for. I'd stay on the outside for the first two rounds. Take as little damage as possible. And in the third round grind down Ricci until the end of the fight. We sparred hard. We boxed. And we did a lot of strength and conditioning drills. Considering what I went through in the Davis fight, and considering how hard I trained, I knew no matter what happened my preparedness would shine.

Before you fight, there's a tense silence filling the air of the warm-up room with uncertainty, especially if you're the main event of the night. Because by that time the other fighters and coaches have cleared out. A friend or a family member might pop in to say hello once in a while. But for the most part, you're forced to sit there with your thoughts. So there I sat with my coaches, and my son, Jube, waiting for the door to open and the ring usher to call my name. There was no adding anything. I either had what I needed, or I didn't.

As I sat and looked around at the cut-up hands wraps and bloody gauze and empty beer cans lying on the floor, I could hear the muffled sounds of the crowd. The door opened. The noise grew and a voice from a man said, "You're next, Chris." I rose to my feet. I hugged and kissed my son and told him I loved him. And my team and I made our way out of the warm-up room and into the crowd of spectators who'd come to see me slay Canadian number three.

I saw the crowd first. Fans cheered my name. As I walked toward the ring I could make out the faces of friends sitting in the front row. The energy was live. I went to my corner and kneeled down to say a few words. And I walked up the stairs and jumped over the top rope. My feet touched the canvas and the crowd cheered. I felt alive. I felt at home. Everything was familiar. The lights. The church basement. The crowd. Everything that is, except for Alex Ricci. When I looked over at Ricci he was standing in his corner wearing mixed martial arts shorts. Why would Ricci, a traditional Muay Thai fighter, be wearing mma shorts? I tried to put the thought in the back of my head.

The bell rang for the first round and we touched gloves. Ricci came out with a furious pace. He was nothing like we expected. He didn't have a Thai style at all. He had more of a Dutch kick boxing style. Pop. Pop. Pop. His punches came in numbers. Whack. He finished off with strong low kicks. "What the hell is happening here? We didn't train for this." Ricci spent time in Thailand. His teammates, his gym, they were traditional Muay Thai stylists. Why was he not following suit? By the end of the first round he damaged me, physically and psychologically.

"You gotta check the low kick," Jason kept telling me. But Ricci set his kicks up with speedy punches. And when I did hit him with kicks and punches, I couldn't faze him. He stood his ground. That's the mental side of fighting which took me years to figure out. And that's where fighters win or lose. Because fighting is about who's more effective at hiding the pain. Fighting is about who could show less emotion. And Ricci was winning the physical and psychological war.

In the second round I found my distance and scored with body kicks. In the clinch we stalemated. But once we went back to the outside Ricci was winning all the exchanges. He continued to punish me with punches and low kicks. My legs started going. And I was still taking punches to the head. I wasn't sure how much more my body could handle.

Jason always told me I was a five round fighter. I usually didn't wake up until the third round. And then I went out to seek and destroy and put on a show for the crowd. But because Ricci had punished me in the first two rounds, I stepped into the third round empty. And Ricci made me pay. Somehow, by the leather of my gloves, I escaped the third round.

As I sat on the stool in the corner going into the fourth round I thought about my fight with Oliver Davis. "I've been here. Now I gotta find a way to come back. I gotta do something." But what could I do? I lost three rounds. This guy was chopping my legs up. He was pounding me with punches. And he was beating me in my hometown. On top of that I ran out of gas. And my head wasn't clear. "Keep those heavy body kicks going," Jason said. And he disappeared back into the shadows of the corner and I walked out under the lights of the ring.

In the fourth round Ricci and I exchanged techniques and I did what Jason said. I hit him in the body with a powerful kick to the liver. For the first time in the fight I stopped him. With pure will I pushed forward, looking for the shovel hook to his body. I went high, landing with heavy hands to his head. I had him backed into the ropes. "This is it. I got him. I'm gonna knock him out." As he came off the ropes I lined him up for a right rear uppercut. By this point the pain had overtaken my body. I stood on wobbly legs. I couldn't see everything in front me. But my heart carried me through. I dug my feet down into the canvas and loaded up for a rear uppercut with everything I had.

There's something uncertain about the sound of silence in the warm-up room before a fight, because at that point it's still anyone's night. But when the sound of silence comes after a fight, there's nothing uncertain about it. I tried to come to my senses but I couldn't push myself off the canvas. My eyes were still trying to refocus. And when they did, that's when I noticed the eyes upon me. Some wore looks of sorrow. Others wore looks of disappointment. I looked over at Jason and I could see the sadness pouring out of him. As a coach you never want to show too much. But Jason and I had history. And I could read his eyes as well as he could read mine. "What happened?" I asked the referee. "You're going to have to watch the tape," he said.

Before Ricci knocked me out I remember loading up for the uppercut. The rest I saw on tape. I saw how he used his experience to bait me in. I saw how I overcommitted with my rear uppercut and left my chin in the air as an easy target for him. I saw as he bounced off the ropes and threw a stiff right cross, landing on my jaw. And I watched my body crumble like a tower of playing cards as I went face first into the canvas.

Confidence can get you almost anywhere in life. But competence gets you through it. Competence gets people through most difficult situations. Getting knocked out was hard to accept. I thought I was going to claim my third victory over Siam #1 and their fighters. I thought I was going to make my mark as one of the best in the middleweight division. But instead, I felt like I let New York City down.

ROUND FOUR: COMING BACK

CHAPTER EIGHT
THE ROAD BACK

"It's a funny thing coming home. Nothing changes. Everything looks the same, feels the same, even smells the same. You realize what has changed is you."
- F. Scott Fitzgerald

I received the call from Mildred while I was working at New York Sports Club. We hadn't been together in five years, so Mildred wanting to move to North Carolina didn't bother me. But I didn't expect her move to come so soon. "What about Jube?" I said. "Who's he gonna stay with?" Mildred suggested that Jube go with her down south, but there was no way I could let Jube out of my life. First, I still wanted to be the father I never had. And I couldn't be Jube's father from halfway up the East Coast. Second, what kind of opportunities would Jube have down south? New York had better schools. He'd have more career opportunities in the future. And on top of that, everything he knew—his friends and most of his family—was in New York. Mildred and I came to an agreement after a couple weeks. She decided to let Jube stay with me under one condition, that I took care of Jube like she would've, and that Jube make regular trips to North Carolina to see her.

The first few months of having Jube with me were challenging. Not because of Jube, but because of my work and fight training schedule. I trained my first client at New York Sports Club at 6AM. Every weekday I woke Jube up at 4:30AM and brought him with me. My manager knew my situation and was cool with Jube being there. So Jube would hang out or nap in the gym. After my first client I brought Jube to school, which was a few blocks away. Then I went back to the gym to train my clients or I went to Church Street Boxing Gym to train myself. When I finished at Church Street I picked Jube up from School and headed back to New York Sports Club until 8PM. And Jube and I grabbed dinner in Astoria, where we lived like two bachelors. The schedule was tough on both of us, but I understood in the end Jube would learn the value of sacrifice and hard work.

This went on five days a week. I didn't have any clients on the weekends, so Jube and I spent our time hanging out in parks or eating at restaurants. I tried to relate to him the lessons I learned though life. I suppose I compared our father and son relationship to the Japanese story of the Lone Wolf and Cub. I looked at myself like Ogami Ittō, the shogun executioner who was accused of using a dōtanuki battle sword and was kicked out of the clan. He took the path of an assassin, and with his three-year-old son, sought out revenge on the clan that rejected him. I was the Lone Wolf. And Jube was the Cub.

But even the quiet times we shared were meaningful. My father never watched movies with me. He never cooked meals for me. Even if I wasn't interacting with Jube, I like to think being there for him if he needed me said enough. But I also knew, for that matter, Jube needed more than what I could give him.

Relationships are a lot like fights. Some of them go the distance. Some of them don't. I was happy to make a name for myself as a knockout fighter whose fights didn't last. But I wasn't happy being a single dad who couldn't hold down a relationship. I wanted to settle down, because I was too rough around the edges to raise Jube on my own. A young man needs balance. He needs to know there's more to life than fighting. Years of fighting don't lend to being soft. And being soft, I thought, was a sign of weakness.

I dated, but I was selective, because women who complained about superficial nonsense bothered me. And for a while, those were the women I attracted. They talked about how much they hated their jobs. They had no vision or drive. I felt like they'd be the baggage weighing me down on my journey through life, not the woman walking next to me on the path. Besides, I had a comeback to focus on. I couldn't pick anyone else up off the canvas while I was still picking myself up.

In my fight with Alex Ricci I tore my ACL, MCL, and meniscus. I didn't have health insurance so I hobbled around the gym and at work. I wore a knee brace and avoided training with my left leg. But after six months my knee still bothered me. So I went to the doctor and he suggested operating on it. I didn't like the idea of surgery, though. If I was going to get cut open, it was going to happen in a fight, not on an operating table. I went to another doctor for a second opinion and he said the same thing. But I knew there had to be another way.

Then I met a sports medicine doctor who said I could rehab my knee without surgery. But he said the rehab would take a long time. With his blessings, I sought out a physical therapist and began rehabbing my knee. I saw the therapist three times a week, and between the massage therapy, exercises and stretches, electric stimulation, and acupuncture, I was able to box again after six months.

My time off, though, taught me to slow down and appreciate life's lessons. In the past, I moved through accomplishments and setbacks without giving myself much time to extract the nuggets of wisdom. With so much down time, I began to appreciate my loss to Ricci. He was the Edwin of my professional fight career. I could've taken them both more seriously, but I didn't. I assumed I was a tough kid from Queens when I got smashed by Edwin, like I assumed Ricci would show up with a traditional Muay Thai style. Both of those instances showed me I couldn't control the world. But I could control how I thought about the world.

If I was ever going to see my name listed among the greatest names in American Muay Thai I needed to change. I needed to cultivate patience. I needed to be more calculated. And I needed to stop fighting off of emotion. Not to take anything away from Ricci, because he was the better man that night, but my carelessness got me knocked out. Putting the fault on me, I was confident my carelessness was something Jason and I could change. And for the next few months we poured our resources into transforming myself into an adaptable and calculated fighter. In the meantime, Justin Blair sought out a comeback fight for me. And within due time, he found me a fight against Jay Ellis.

During fight training I usually arrived at Church Street Boxing Gym before Jason. The gym was on Park Place in the Tribeca area of Manhattan, in the bottom of a five-story building. To get down to the gym, you had to descend a metal staircase and walk through a narrow brick corridor. From there the gym opened up, as if you were in the belly of some boxing megalith. Murals of Muhammad Ali and Joe Louis and other legends covered the wall. And alongside speed bags and double-end bags, heavy bags lined the interior.

One night, waiting for Jason to show up, I was hammering away on the heavy bag. I kept a close eye on the doorway, expecting Jason to pop in any second. My eyes darted from the bag to the door and back to the bag. When I looked up again, through the corridor emerged a girl, a girl I never saw at the gym. She wore a long dress that flowed with each of her movements. Her hair was brown and her eyes sparkled. And she gave off an aura that lit the gritty backdrop of Church Street. She was, I suppose, the antithesis of what most people walking into a professional boxing gym look like. I kept my eye on her as she crossed the floor in front of me. She didn't speak to anyone. And no one told her what to do. She jumped on a heavy bag and went to work. I didn't expect her to break a sweat, never mind throw a left hook. "She's gotta be a pro boxer," I thought.

Jason showed up and we went to work. I climbed into the ring and hit pads. But my attention was on the girl hitting the bag. Up until then, I put everything except for Jube aside. My comeback fight was a few weeks out and I didn't want any distractions in my life. I promised myself there'd be no more mistakes in the ring. But there was something about the girl in the dress that kept pulling me in. At the end of the night we saw each other in the hallway and exchanged smiles.

When I went to the gym the next day she showed up again-and the day after. One night while I was leaving the gym I noticed her on the metal staircase ahead of me. I knew I had to say something. But I didn't want to embarrass myself with this pro female fighter. I was never a lady's man, so I said the first thing that came to mind. "No matter what shape you're in these stairs will make you feel outta shape." She smiled.

She told me her name was Sarah. And Sarah dressed so nicely because she owned a vintage clothing store in the city. And I found out, despite working so hard in the gym, she wasn't a professional boxer. I dropped my guard and we talked for a few more minutes. Our conversation was an innocent flirt but it felt great. And although I wanted to get back on my journey through fighting, Sarah had me. I wanted to know more about her.

Church Street Boxing Gym was a fighter's gym. And one of the staples in the gym was a black leather couch, torn to shreds and soaked in years of sweat. The couch felt like a sponge and smelled like a wet, dirty sock. I never expected to woo a woman with my words there. But Sarah and Jube and I sat on the couch after training one night, talking. It was the first time Sarah and I had the chance to talk without interruption, except for Jube pulling at my ears the entire time. I tried to pull myself together and act like an adult while Jube tugged at my lobes. I thought Sarah might think negatively of me, but the opposite was true. Sarah and Jube took to each. She was kind toward Jube. The moment felt so real. I didn't think I'd find a woman so caring toward Jube. But I also wondered how she felt about me. She didn't know I was a single dad. And I didn't know if she was single either.

Thirteen months passed between my loss to Ricci and the night of my comeback fight. But I felt like I never left fighting. I went through the routine of getting my hands wrapped and shadowboxing. And while Jason reminded me of the technical game plan, I reminded myself to stay calculated and adaptable. Out of the corner of my eye I saw Sarah walk into the warm-up room. "How'd she get in here?" I thought. "Did she come in to see me?" I tried to play it cool. Then she walked over to see her friend who was fighting the same night. We made eye contact and smiled.

People ask me what coming back after a long hiatus from the sport is like. They ask me if I felt uncertain, or fearful of the man standing across from me. And sure, when faced with great challenges these emotions surface in all of us, even us fighters. But going into my comeback fight I was concerned only about redemption. And Jay Ellis, the wild and strong and fearless fighter, stood between redemption and me like a gatekeeper.

When I entered the ring I reminded myself once again of my intentions. I walked around the inside perimeter of the ring and did the wai kru. And then I returned to my corner. Jason took off my mongkon and I turned to face Ellis standing across from me. He was bouncing on his toes, staring back. He looked ready for war. But so was I. "We gotta wait," a voice said from outside of the ring. I looked around in confusion. The ref came over and told me there were no medics on scene. So we couldn't fight yet. I learned later on, in the bout before ours, a fighter was knocked out and paramedics had to bring him to the hospital. So there we stood, Ellis and I, waiting for the medics to get back to the venue. Up until then, I never stood in a ring for that long without doing something. And for some reason, nerves probably, I started dancing to Cypress Hill playing over the sound system. I pumped my glove up in the air over and over again like I was pulling a light string.

When the first bell rang Ellis came out aggressive, trying to keep me on the back foot and cut off the ring. But I used my footwork to evade his wild movements. In the middle of the first round I caught him with a straight right, sending him to the canvas. He stood back up, and again he stormed forward with an unshakeable aggression and wildness. Like a matador toying a bull, I baited him in and sidestepped, popping him with punches, crushing his legs with kicks. A moment later I caught him again. He went down and couldn't answer the ref's count.

The first round knockout win was bittersweet. I dismantled Jay Ellis in dominating fashion. I proved to myself and to fight fans I learned from my mistakes and became a more calculated fighter. But I wished the fight lasted longer. I wanted more time in the ring to knock off the rust, to get my fighting legs back under me. But at least I was back home, on top of the canvas and under the lights of Friday Night Fights.

I stepped out of the ring and friends and family embraced me. Everyone talked about celebrating. I rushed to the locker room to wash up and we went to a restaurant in the city. At the restaurant a mass of friends and fans surrounded me, some coming and some going, most of them congratulating me on my win. But my attention was elsewhere. I looked over and saw Sarah in the crowd. She looked over at me. I wanted to talk to her and I could tell she wanted to talk to me, but the ocean of people between us made reaching her impossible. The crowd in the restaurant dwindled and I made my way toward her. "Let's get out of here," I said. And we walked through the East Village until three in the morning. Afterwards we went to a diner for coffee. We talked about religion, raising kids, and fighting, all the stuff lacking from my dates with previous women. At the end of the night we said our goodbyes but made plans to meet again the next day.

CHAPTER NINE
THE DRAGON OF INSIGNIFICANCE

"Nothing in the world can take the place of persistence. Talent will not; nothing is more common than unsuccessful men with talent. Genius will not; unrewarded genius is almost a proverb. Education alone will not; the world is full of educated derelicts. Persistence and determination alone are omnipotent. The slogan 'Press On' has solved and always will solve the problem of the human race."
- John Calvin Coolidge

Justin Blair held a charity event under the Friday Night Fight's banner on November 2, 2009. He invited me to come down and watch. In the main event, Sean Hinds, a British fighter living in New York, was fighting an old adversary of mine, Alex Ricci. Hinds was a reputable and respected fighter well versed in the art of Muay Thai. He traveled all over the world to compete and was climbing the middleweight ranks.

The Hinds and Ricci fight interested me for many reasons. As a fan I knew they'd put on a good show. As a fighter who lost to Ricci, I was curious how Hinds would fair against him. And in the back of my head I was hoping to meet Hinds in the ring one day. Needless to say I sat and watched with a keen eye. And Hinds made a statement from round one. He pummeled Ricci's leg with low kicks. Hinds caught Ricci with a hard straight right, dropping my former opponent. A fight's a fight, and I knew anything was possible. But Hinds' performance surprised me. Hinds went on to win the decision, having his way with Ricci for most of the fight. Ricci limped out of the ring. I couldn't help but watch in awe. Ricci was my dragon. And Hinds slew Ricci with ease.

After Hinds' performance at the charity event people started talking about the possibility of him and me fighting. After all, we were the two best middleweights in New York City. Diehard fans wanted to see the fight. I wanted the fight. I knew Hinds would take the fight. But before Hinds fought on Justin Blair's charity event, he fought for Simon Burgess and Steve Milles or fought abroad. I headlined Friday Night Fights. I was loyal to

Justin so I couldn't fight Hinds under another promotion.

I kept putting the idea in Justin's head that I wanted to fight Hinds next. I wanted to fight the best. And Hinds was the man to beat. He was a worthy opponent and after seeing what he did to Ricci, fighting Hinds would be an incredible challenge. I waited and waited for an answer from Justin Blair. And then it happened. Justin sent me an email asking if I wanted to fight Hinds in 2010.

Hinds' team and my team both agreed on a fight date and purse. The event, which Justin Blair billed as the biggest Muay Thai show in New York City, was going to take place at the Lexington Armory in Manhattan. Two thousand five hundred people would attend. To top it off, the winner of the fight would be the first ever North American WKA Super-Middleweight Champion.

Word spread through the Muay Thai community that Hinds and I were going to fight. And it became the topic of debate at most gyms in New York City. Hinds, after all, had a powerful reputation and people thought I didn't stand a chance. I understood because on paper the fight looked easy for Hinds. I was the local fighter; he traveled the world. I was the underdog; he had the experience. I lost to Ricci in devastating fashion; he devastated Ricci. But I had something people hadn't added to the unbalanced equation—heart. My entire career I was the underdog. This is where I thrived.

Up until the moment I signed the contract to fight Hinds, I spent my career fighting off the out-of-towners who came to test my mettle in New York City. But this fight was different. Because after the final bell rang and the judges made their decision, neither one of us was returning home. New York City was our home. And only one of us would wear the middleweight strap. I kept playing the Ricci fight over and over in my head during training, but for the right reasons. Knowing Hinds beat Ricci didn't scare me. It fueled me. I had intentions now, and a game plan.

I was never a ball of energy before my fights. But like most fighters, nerves came and went. To offset the occasional bout of nerves I listened to music in the warm-up room. My fight with

Sean Hinds was no different, although my selection of music was. I popped in my ear buds and let the sounds of Salsa take my feet wherever they wanted to go. My mind drifted with the rhythms of the clave and the conga and the campaña. And I thought back to what I read about Bruce Lee, and how he was a proficient Cha-Cha dancer, and how his philosophies on self-expression gave meaning and purpose to my life as a fighter. Because fighting was one way for me to express myself, to express what "Mr. Classic" represented. And I represented the idea that you can hunt down your dreams, whether you're stepping into an office or stepping into a ring.

The night closed in on the inevitable. And with each passing fight before mine, I became more hardened and ready for war. Jason wrapped my hands. And with a few fights left, he slipped the gloves over the casts on my fists and I knew my purpose. He pulled the laces tighter and wrapped them in knots. The gloves became extensions of who I was, extensions of my body, ready to inflict whatever damage I could to Hinds, but also extensions of my soul. In a way, they were the brushes I used to paint my masterpiece on the canvas of life.

The fight drew closer. I could smell the menthol from muscle liniment in the air and feel it burn in my lungs. I tried to stay hydrated by sipping water, but my mouth felt like I was chewing on sand. I shadowboxed to keep my body fresh. Jason, Jube, and the rest of my team sat without speaking, watching and thinking and waiting. Jason looked at me with the same smile he wore before each fight, a smile that stunk of nerves but rang with excitement. "You're next, Chris." The voice shouldn't have come as a surprise, but it did. And the ring escort ushered us upstairs and into the doorway separating the hallway and the arena of Lexington Armory. "Wait here until your name is called," he said.

I often wonder if my father had shown any interest in me, would I have turned out to be the person I am today? I can't answer the question in good faith. But I do know growing up without his support or love made me feel insignificant. And since then, I've chased significance my entire life. Fighting was one way for me to find it. And I found it in the doorway of Lexington Armory. When the ring announcer called my name and the echoes of his voice fell on my ears and the crowd erupted, I felt significant. When I took one step through the doorway, over the threshold of all that was and walked toward all that might be, I felt significant. And when I heard the chants of the crowd calling my name, calling out "CROM," calling out "Mr. Classic," again and again, I felt significant.

With my chest and my chin high and my spirit even higher I marched forward, moving through the crowd to the sound of the Conan the Barbarian theme song—my walkout music for each of my fights. "It's go time," I kept telling myself. "Time to prove who's best." We walked from the shadows of the Armory to the center of the arena; the ring and the reality drew closer, the lights brighter, the crowd louder. I made my way around the ring toward my corner. Fans in the front row pumped their fists, yelling, "You got this, Chris!" I nodded my head. I took a knee at the steps leading up to the ring and I visualized my ring entrance. I walked up the steps, climbed over the ropes, and footed myself in the ring, shuffling sideways. I made my way to the opposite side of the ring and turned to Hinds and gave him a pound.

"May the universe bring me victory and bring me safely back to my family and friends," I repeated as I walked to each corner and performed the wai kru. I felt the heat of the lights and the hold of the crowd's eyes upon me. I felt Hinds and his corner men watching me move. I often refer to this moment as the fight before the fight, the moment when the trainers and other fighter size you up. They look for flaws in your posture and composure. They look for signs of uncertainty. I say fighting is like the biggest lie, because you're trying to convince the crowd and your opponent and yourself that you're not nervous. In the fight you lie when you're hurt, hiding the pain. You lie when you're tired. But on the other end fighting is the ultimate truth. Fighting is the rawest expression of your mind, body, and soul. Whatever you lack gets exposed, whether it's timing, balance, skill, or courage. In the ring you face everything you conceal as a lie or believe to be true. And after the opening bell rang both Hinds and I would face our truths.

"Go out there and have fun," Jason said. After seven years of training and fighting together we knew we did the work in the gym. Now it was about having fun. When the bell rang Hinds and I met in the middle of the ring and touched gloves. I attacked first, trying to send a message to Hinds that I meant business. For the better of two rounds we warred back and forth. And in the second round, he caught me. My legs buckled and straightened again. I told myself there'd be no way I was going down. This wasn't going to be a replay of my fight with Alex Ricci. I hid my pain and pressed on.

In the clinch I dominated Hinds and nullified his low kick attack. And when he threw his hook to my head and body I countered with one of my own. I started attacking his right side with my left kicks. I deterred him from being offensive. Once he slowed down I used my push kicks to keep him off balance. And toward the end of the fight, I landed a body kick, causing his mouthpiece to hang out of his mouth. He backtracked and I had him pinned against the ropes. I wasn't sure if he was baiting me. I popped my jab in his face for good measure.

The bell rang and I knew I did enough to win the fight. His boxing was good. But this was Muay Thai, and I did a better job of showing and landing all my weapons. But when fights go the distance and you leave them for the judges to decide you never know what to expect. Jason took off my gloves and I went to the center of the ring to wait for the announcement along with Hinds. David Diamante, the ring announcer, announced the first judge's score: forty-nine to forty-six for me. He announced the second judge's score: forty-eight to forty-seven, in favor of Hinds. We waited and the tension rose. David Diamante read the last scorecard. "And forty-eight to forty-seven, to your winner, by split decision, and the new WKA Professional North American Men's Muay Thai Super-Middleweight Champion," he paused, "Chris, Mr. Classic, Romulo!"

If having my name called out before I walked to the ring made me feel significant, then having my name called out as the new super-middleweight champion made me feel extraordinary. Not because I won, and not because I won a title or New York City bragging rights, but because, for that moment, I won a fight much bigger than the one taking place in the ring. For the first time in my career I looked over and saw Jube crying tears of joy. I was to Jube what my father never was to me. I picked up my son, and with him sitting on my arm, we walked around the ring, him raising his hand, and me raising mine.

ROUND FIVE: GOING THE DISTANCE

CHAPTER TEN
MARRIAGE

"So, I love you because the entire universe conspired to help me find you."
- Paulo Coehlo

For as long as I could remember my mom wanted me to settle down with someone she called "a nice Filipino girl," which I never understood. Because when I was younger my mom did everything she could to Americanize me. She moved me out of what seemed like the only Queens neighborhood with Filipinos living in it. She only spoke English to me. She fed me American food. Even if I did meet a "nice Filipino girl," I had no way to relate to her. I could, however, relate to Sarah. And since my fight with Jay Ellis, Sarah and I were inseparable. But I wondered whether or not my mom would accept Sarah.

One day, around Christmas in 2008, my friend Gabe had a party in The Ville at his house, which was across the street from my parent's house. Sarah asked me if she could meet my mother and father. But knowing my family, I was hesitant to bring Sarah over to their house. Sarah grew upset because she thought I was ashamed of her. Or she thought my mom wouldn't accept her because she wasn't a Filipina. But truth be told, I was worried that Sarah wouldn't understand my dysfunctional family because from what I gathered she had a loving and supportive upbringing.

Six months passed before I felt comfortable introducing Sarah to my mom. By this time I already met Sarah's parents and brothers and sisters. And I felt welcomed by her family. But would my mom welcome Sarah into ours? Sarah met my brother, Andrew, and his wife, Mitzi, first. My brother and his wife were always there for me and spent a lot of time with Jube. They knew finding someone who would accept both of us was important to me. So meeting someone like Sarah—who got along with Jube so well—pleased my brother and his wife.

I arranged for Sarah to meet my mom next. And except for my father, we all went to eat at a Cuban restaurant. My mom took to Sarah, which gave me some relief. But my mom, who echoed similar sentiments as Sarah's parents, worried about Jube. If it didn't work out between Sarah and me, Jube would suffer the loss of a meaningful relationship. But the thought never crossed our minds. Sarah and I knew we wanted to build our lives together. Sarah accepted Jube, and she wanted to be there for him as well.

After I met Sarah's family and Sarah met my family we started looking for houses to move into. Sarah told me about her friend, John Cori, who owned a house in a place called Rockaway Beach. I never heard of Rockaway Beach before. I knew about the Far Rockaways from the nineties hip-hop group, Third Base. And I knew about the projects out there. I was a little skeptical. But I agreed to go take a look anyway. Up until then, the furthest I ventured out to the east side of Queens was Cross Bay Boulevard. So when we crossed over the Cross Bay Veterans Memorial Bridge and hit the Rockaway peninsula, I couldn't believe I was looking at a wildlife preservation and a bay. I was born and raised in Queens, and it took Sarah, a Jersey Girl, to show me the nature that existed in the eastern corner of the borough.

John Cori's house was a Victorian Era home, complete with a wooden staircase and the trimmings of antiquity. The house was also about one hundred and fifty feet away from the beach. The house and neighborhood were a stark contrast from the cookie-cutter homes I grew up around in The Ville, where the only water I saw was from the puddles that gathered after rainstorms.

It was also mid-January when we went to look at the house. The second floor was vacant, which meant the heat was off. We roughed the night on a blowup mattress because we wanted to see the neighborhood in the morning. When we woke up the next day, John Cori took us to the beach. And despite what I originally thought, seeing the neighborhood in the daytime wasn't a strong selling point. Vacant buildings lined the boulevard. There was a single pizzeria. A sheet of ice covered the entire boardwalk.

And the boardwalk ran along a beach we could only use part of the year. But right on the boardwalk was a brand new skateboarding park. And Jube loved to skateboard. I looked at Sarah. "Let's do this," I said. There was something about the old home, the beach town that didn't seem to fit into Queens Borough, the skate park. I could see us raising a family there, integrating ourselves into the community.

In May 2009 we moved into the second floor of the Victorian home, and the ghost town came to life. The surf shop opened up. Locals and visitors animated the once lifeless boardwalk. I began to feel like we made a great decision. But we only enjoyed Rockaway Beach part of the time. Sarah still worked in the city. Jube went to school in the city. And I trained clients and trained myself in the city too. The travel was becoming too much for us, so we started to devise a plan that would let us work and live in our Rockaway Beach community.

While Sarah and I put our minds together on a future business plan, I formed a plan of my own. As a kid and teenager, I watched my mom and dad live out an unhappy existence together. Most of my friends came from broken homes too. My relationship with Jube's mom failed. For a long time the idea of marriage turned me off. But when Sarah came along, everything changed. We had a connection people go their entire lives without finding. I opened up to her in ways I never did in past relationships. For all I wasn't, for all I lacked, she provided. Where I was too rough, she smoothed me out. Where I was too tough, she softened me up. And where I thought I could be the mom and dad for Jube while he was under my roof, she showed me otherwise. As a fighter and as a man I needed balance. And Sarah was that balance. But she also opened her heart to Jube, and Jube opened his heart to her. Knowing this, I wanted to spend my life with Sarah. I wanted to ask for her hand in marriage.

I had one challenge with asking Sarah to marry me though. Her father was a successful cardiologist. Her mom was a nurse. Her brothers were doctors. One of Sarah's sisters was a nurse practitioner in a women's cancer unit. The other married a successful businessman. And on the inside they seemed so loving and generous and accepting—a contrast to my family, who fought and argued and found shelter not from love, but from detachment.

Needless to say, asking Sarah's father for his daughter's hand intimidated me. I was rough around the edges. I grew up on the streets. I never took a college class in my life. I didn't have much to offer Sarah aside from my heart and the dreams of where I wanted to take her in life. I regret not doing the noble thing and asking Sarah's father for her hand, but the thoughts of how he'd perceive me churned inside my mind.

Back at Gabe's house during the previous Christmas, I was still hesitant to let Sarah into my life, to show her my family's faults and flaws. But a year passed. There was nothing Sarah didn't know about me. And I wanted to let go of my negative ideas of family and marriage and start over. On Christmas Day I took a knee and asked Sarah to be my wife. Six months later we exchanged vows at St. Rose De Lima Church. Jube was my best man. And my brothers and best friends were my groomsmen. We wore traditional Filipino Barongs, embroidered shirts considered to be the national attire of the Philippines. It was the closest I felt to my Filipino culture. And I loved sharing that with Sarah, the woman who balanced me, who pushed me to be a better man, who, as I learned, would stand in my corner and face life's greatest challenges with me.

CHAPTER ELEVEN
HANGING UP THE GLOVES

"The deepest secret is that life is not a process of discovery, but a process of creation. You are not discovering yourself, but creating yourself anew. Seek, therefore, not to find out who you are, seek to determine who you want to be."
- Neal Donald Walsch

As a fighter, I wanted to travel the world. I wanted to fight in places I only read or heard about. I wanted to experience life and broaden my perspective. But as my professional career funneled toward that narrowing hole of possibility, I grew to accept my fate—that I came long before the lights. And in some way I carried through the dark ages a sport unknown, in a city known to the world. It was a place where I carved my legacy, where many fighters and non-fighters alike came to test their mettle. But New York City, nonetheless, was a city I wanted to escape.

I fought for Justin Blair and Friday Night Fights for a decade. And although Justin looked after me like one of his own, I knew he didn't want me to fight on anyone else's show. From a promoter's perspective, I was an investment in his business. And Jason was busy training fighters at Church Street Boxing Gym. To expect either Justin or Jason to get me fights outside of New York City was unrealistic. But time and age were getting to me. And with each passing fight I felt my body shedding the fighter within. My timing slowed. My intentions calmed. And the fire that once fueled my fighting spirit lay in glowing embers.

I felt the physical changes of being in the ring when I fought a tough Russian by the name of Alexander Lavrushin. Lavrushin was a Kyokushin fighter training in Philadelphia at the time. He was young and hungry and when we met at the weigh-ins I could sense he meant business. Usually before each of my fights I laughed and joked around with my opponents. But Lavrushin looked at me with eyes like a shark. And in the ring he hunted me down like one too. He knocked me down early in the fight, and in true Romulo fashion I jumped up and waved my fist in the air, letting everyone know I was still in the fight. Lavrushin went on to win a decision, but the loss was tough to put my family through.

I used to say age slowed me down the night I fought Lavrushin. But the truth was, my relationship with Jube was falling apart. I was so focused on building the gym and training for my fight that I wasn't spending much time with him. And to top it off, Sarah was pregnant with my second son. Jube probably felt, for the first time ever, he'd become second in line because Jube and I lived together for so long. When he told Sarah and me that he wanted to move to North Carolina with his mom, my world fell apart.

At a loss, Sarah and I decided to see Dr. David Jones, a family therapist. And he uncovered what we thought, that the coming baby worried Jube, and that Jube missed his family down south. We sat down with Jube and told him the benefits of staying up North as opposed to moving to North Carolina. We told him we would like him to stay with us, but the choice was his to make. And no matter what choice he made, we'd respect his decision. Jube thought the move over for a few days and in the end he decided to stay with us in Rockaway. Fight training is hard enough. But when you find out your son wants to leave you, fighting gets harder. I don't blame him in any way for the loss to the Russian. I blame me for not being there when Jube needed me most. If I was there when Jube needed me, this wouldn't have happened, and maybe I would've fought better. But I didn't. And I couldn't leave the fight game on that note. I knew I had one more fight in me.

Throughout my amateur and professional fight career I had one manager, back when I was thinking of transitioning to mixed martial arts. Otherwise, I worked with Justin Blair and Jason and together we decided on who and when I fought. The relationship worked out for all of us. Justin brought in the crowd. Jason trained me. And I stayed busy, headlining most of the Friday Night Fight venues. But I still itched to fight, even once, outside of New York. So in 2011 I recruited a manager, Kevin Lillis.

Kevin worked in real estate and had an incredible gift of

gab. For all I lacked in outgoing and extroverted behavior, he made up for with his personable demeanor. He also understood what I was worth as a fighter, and he appreciated the effort I put into the sport. Kevin would show up to my fights with two-dozen high rollers to cheer me on. And, because of the contrast in our lifestyles, he lived through my fighting. He'd make the perfect manager, I thought. And my intuition was right. Within a few weeks he was talking to one of the fastest rising Muay Thai promotions in North America, Lion Fight Promotions.

Right around the time I reached out to Lillis to get me a fight outside of New York, the American Muay Thai community was splitting at the seams. Chaz Mulkey, a Muay Thai fighter from the West Coast, went on record to say East Coast professional fighters were amateurs at best. With his statement, Mulkey stirred up a lot of controversy. But the controversy needed to happen. Back in 2011 elbows in Muay Thai were illegal in New York. And Chaz, along with a list of other West Coast fighters, figured since we didn't fight with elbows, we shouldn't call ourselves professional fighters.

But Chaz was pointing his fingers at the wrong people. For one, fighters on the East Coast wanted nothing more than to use elbows. But the regulating bodies were holding us back from doing so. And two, I, along with a bunch of other fighters, spent years grinding out professional careers, taking on whoever they put in front of us. When Chaz called out the East Coast, I felt like he was talking to me. And I needed to step up. I wasn't going to let anyone talk down about our fighters.

Kevin Lillis reached out to Christine Toledo of Lion Fight. And we began talks of an East Coast versus West Coast fight card, with Chaz Mulkey and I fighting each other. The fight was everything I wanted. Fighting outside of New York City was going to be great. But showing Mulkey I was a game fighter was going to be even better. Negotiations failed, though. We couldn't agree on a fight weight that suited both of us. Chaz couldn't come up in weight and fight at one hundred and sixty-five pounds. And I couldn't get any lower. I spent my entire career fighting at super-middleweight. I'd have to cut a limb off to get any lower. With that, my chances of fighting on Lion Fight dwindled.

Then Kevin Lillis called me. "We got someone," he said. "Shawn Yarborough." I was no stranger to the name. I met Yarborough down in Virginia when I was an amateur. I remember shaking his hand and watching my hand disappear into his. I remember looking up at him. And I was thankful we didn't fight in the same weight class. "Let's do it," I told Lillis. I wanted to send a message to anyone on the West Coast who questioned our ability and competence. And I wanted everyone to know I'd fight whoever the promoter gave me at my weight class or within my weight range. Yarborough fought at one hundred and seventy-five pounds. But we agreed to meet at one hundred and sixty-eight pounds.

Yarborough had the height and reach advantage. And he hit like a truck. So Jason and I worked on not standing in front of Shawn long enough for him to tag me. During fight training, I reached out to Derek Riddick, who fought Shawn Yarborough a few years back and beat him. Riddick told me Yarborough didn't like to clinch. And in the clinch Riddick found his own success. I kept that in the back of my mind. Because looking back on my fight with Ricci—even Cerrone—I knew anything could happen. Fighters change gyms. They evolve. I wasn't sure what to expect from Yarborough. But I knew what he could expect from me.

I fought for Friday Night Fights for so long that I internalized my pre-fight rituals. But being in Nevada, fighting under a different promotion, my emotions swung between fear and courage. I didn't have the comforts of home before the fight, if such a thing existed. For one, this was the first time in my career—aside from Thailand—I was fighting without Jube in my corner. And to be honest, his presence kept me calm. Having him by my side reminded me why I was fighting. And two, for the last seven fights Sarah was with me. Now she was back home, without me, thirty-six weeks pregnant.

I walked out to the ring and the crowd was silent. No cheers. No shouts of "CROM" or "Mr. Classic" or "Chris" or any other moniker I went by. I saw no familiar faces, only empty stares. The walk from the warm-up room to the ring was lonely. But at the same time I basked in being the out-of-towner for once.

The pressure was on Yarborough now. The West Coast fighters called us out, and we stepped up without hesitation, ready to prove our worth on their soil.

Going into the ring I already knew the fighters couldn't perform the wai kru. This in itself threw me off because I did the wai kru before each of my fights, dating back to my days as an amateur. And for the talk about East Coast fighters not doing "real" Muay Thai, I found it funny we weren't allowed to partake in one of the biggest traditions of Muay Thai. But it didn't matter. I wasn't there to dance; I was there to duel.

Jason removed my mongkon, said a few words of encouragement, and patted me on the shoulder. The bell rang and Yarborough and I touched gloves. Like I expected, Shawn stayed on the outside, using his long reach and keeping his jab in my face. I stayed busy, finding a way to close the distance and get inside. And once I had him in the clinch I learned what Derek Riddick had already told me: Yarborough was big. He was powerful. But inside the clinch I was stronger. I imposed my will and dumped him on the canvas more than a handful of times. He rose back up and again we locked horns. I swam my gloves through his guard and cracked him in the face with my elbow. After four rounds I thought I secured the win. For safe measure, I went out in the last round and stayed dominant. I was sharp and energized until the final bell. Yarborough looked exhausted.

I did what I could to win over the judges, but I knew the nature of the fight game. Pulling off a decision win in Yarborough's backyard was going to be hard. Yarborough and I stood in the middle of the ring and waited for the judges' scores to come in. The first judge announced the fight in my favor. The second judge announced the fight for Yarborough. The third and final judge announced the fight for Yarborough. My first reaction was disappointment.

In fighting a win is the culmination of the hard work, the months spent in the gym, the injuries put aside, and the time sacrificed from family. And in fighting, judges' decisions are opinions, opinions that don't take into account the personal sacrifice leading up to the fight. And when your hand isn't raised after the final bell, you forget. You forget fighting isn't about the decision. As long as you're proud of what you did, as long as you prove to yourself, to your opponent, and to your fans you belong there, nothing else matters. When the ring announcer read the final judge's decision the crowd booed. When I walked out of the ring and back to the warm-up room I heard the sound of scattered cheers.

After the fight Nathan Aripez of Muay Thai Authority interviewed me. He asked me what I thought about the decision. Maybe he, like so many others, expected me to talk down about the experience, to play into the whole East Coast versus West Coast debacle. But instead, I thanked Lion Fight and I thanked Shawn Yarborough. And I even thanked Chaz Mulkey, because I wanted to fight outside of New York City. Chaz stirred up controversy between coasts and gave a thirty-six year old hometown fighter like me the chance to get out and see the world.

Fighting is a young man's game. Older men can fight and find success. But the process isn't easy. Being a fighter is being an entertainer. You have to put on a good performance for the crowd. And against Yarborough, although finding success with the basics, I didn't do anything spectacular. There were no final-second comebacks. No devastating finishes. I didn't display anything fight fans knew me for in the past. I never wanted to be one of those fighters who fought past their prime. I respected guys like Tyson and Holyfield for what they did for boxing. But I found it hard to watch them take beatings at the end of their careers. On the other end, though, I knew how it felt. You can't just walk away from the glory of the fight.

But I was ready to leave the highs and lows of the ring. The highs, those moments of having your hand raised in victory, or bouncing back from defeat. And the lows, those moments when losses test and forge your character. It's hard to walk away from the feeling you get as you make your way to the ring, climb over the top ropes, and stare your opponent in the eyes. Your opponent, nothing more than you, disguised in fear, in challenge, in all you fight not to become. I basked in those moments, because in those moments the fire strengthened my sword. But in my last two fights the fire was no longer there to make stronger my sword. And that was the sign my career as a professional Muay

Thai fighter was coming to an end.

I had a great run. And after I made the decision to retire, following through was easy. I never was wishy-washy. Not inside of the ring, not outside of the ring. I got what I wanted. I fought outside of New York City. And I also got what I needed. And what I needed was to be home, to work on my new gym. To be with Sarah who was pregnant with my second son, and to repair the relationship with my first son, Jube. And I needed to take the fight to the next level. Fighting, first and foremost, was an expression and extension of who I was and what I wanted to give the world. And I knew, after fighting, I'd find a way to continue doing just that.

CHAPTER TWELVE
FROM ONE TO MANY

"The goal is not to strive for a life without struggle, but to sharpen your thoughts to fight the struggle head on."
- Chris Romulo

Underneath the Victorian home, Sarah and I stored a blue beach wagon with giant wheels. And piled in the wagon were kick pads and boxing gloves I collected while setting up different Muay Thai programs throughout the city. Two days a week we rolled the wagon and gear down to the boardwalk and held boot camp Muay Thai classes. Muay Thai didn't exist in Rockaway Beach, so Sarah and I jumped at the chance to introduce the martial art to the community. We used what we had to make the classes fun and challenging. Sarah and I had our students do drills in the sand, run up and down the stairs, hit pads on the boardwalk.

We kept the Muay Thai classes going throughout the summer, and when the fall rolled around the idea of stopping disappointed us. But after our last class Sarah and I were talking with one of our students. She told us about her husband, a Brazilian Jiu Jitsu player, who wanted to go halves with someone on a training space. We felt like we were making progress in the community and wanted to keep our classes going, so we took up the opportunity and split the costs of the space down the middle. The small space was on Old Rockaway Beach Boulevard, nestled between a rundown watering hole and a deli that never escaped the 1950s. It wasn't the best location for foot traffic, but we had faith that if we started a Muay Thai program on the peninsula, people would find out about it. We hung a heavy bag, brought our gear, and held our first official Muay Thai classes. And in six months we outgrew the location.

The small gym showed us what was possible in Rockaway Beach, that people from the community were open to learning a martial art still vague in the eyes of many Americans. And we also tasted what it meant to be a positive impact in the community, for adults and children alike. So Sarah and I wanted to expand our reach. While looking for a bigger space, we came across a storefront on Ninety-Second Street. The storefront was vacant, rundown and in need of a major overhaul. We contacted the landlord and worked out a deal.

In October of 2010 the landlord gave Sarah and me the keys, we recruited some of our students, and we demolished everything inside. For an entire month we hammered, chiseled, banged, broke, knocked down, and built back up the gym how we wanted it. While we stripped away the layers of sheetrock we came across a brick wall. I fell in love with that wall. And for days we worked, exposing every inch of brick. It was a tedious task, but in the end the brick wall gave the gym a unique look and was the perfect place to showcase our trophies, belts, and the gym flag. In November of 2010 Sarah and I were about to open CROM Martial Training. We hung the last of the heavy bags and hit the switches.

Ten thousand dollars. That's how much the electrician would charge Sarah and me for him to run power from the electric pole into the building and rewire the gym. When we rented the space we had no idea there was no electric going into the building. Our landlord was illegally tapping into the neighbors electric. And during renovation we were unknowingly plugging our generator into the extension cord coming from their power supply. Since we were first time commercial space renters, we didn't know our legal rights. We had no idea the responsibility of supplying power fell on the landlord. So we didn't bother to ask him. We knew we had to come up with ten thousand dollars or lose everything we worked hard to build.

With the grand opening already promised and the winter months rolling in, we had to scramble. We bought a kerosene generator to supply us with heat and electric and buy us some time. In the meantime we thought of ways to come up with ten grand. Sarah came up with the idea to ask her parents for the money until we got the gym off the ground and could repay them. I was hesitant because I never liked taking handouts. I was too proud to accept the help. But Sarah convinced me otherwise, and without question, her parents were gracious enough to help us out.

Everything came together in October of 2010 and we grew into a staple of the Rockaway Beach community. In a sense, we became more than a gym; our gym became a sanctuary for the Rockaway youth, the boys and girls with broken spirits who came from broken homes. J.C. was one of those kids. His mom brought him to us when he was eight years old. He was a scrappy little fellow who needed a positive environment and a positive male role model. When J.C. started with us his grades were below average and he acted out in school because his father wasn't in the picture. From day one, though, he showed a lot of heart and passion at the gym.

Around the time J.C.'S mom dropped him off at the gym, we partnered up with the Muaythai Project. The Muaythai Project sponsored at-risk youth to train Muay Thai for no cost as long as the kids produced good grades and stayed motivated at the gym. J.C. won a scholarship with them, which reduced the financial burden on his mom, and he turned his life around. He got himself into Scholar's Academy, one of the best schools in New York City. At the gym, he won national titles under the World Kickboxing Association.

J.C. was everything a coach could want in a student. I loved mentoring him. Let's face it, whenever I looked at J.C. I saw me as an eight-year-old looking back. The lack of a father's presence, the minuscule view of the world, the destructive environment, I lived it. I wanted J.C. and my students in the gym to know there was more to life. I wanted them to know life gives you what you give life. Sarah and I poured our hearts and soul into the gym, and to get students like J.C. in return made the hard work worth our efforts. We found our calling in Rockaway Beach and wanted to grow our family at the gym.

Sarah and I knew we wanted to grow our family at home as well. And in December of 2010 we learned she was pregnant. We needed more space so we moved into a rent-with-the-option-to-buy condo a few doors down from the Victorian home. We had the first floor and basement unit. Sarah, and our soon-to-be son, Gio, and I stayed on the first floor. And Jube stayed in the basement, which we split with a curtain to make his room and the living room.

As a couple getting started with our own business, money was tight. But we tried to make the condo as comfortable as possible, especially for Jube. He had board games and an X-box and a flat screen TV and a futon for his friends to crash on. Sarah painted the basement and decorated it with faux palm trees she picked up from a freelance gig. We also bought a three hundred dollar TV stand, which was a lot of money for us at the time. For days Sarah obsessed over the cost, thinking about how many diapers or Metro cards the money could get us. Funny enough, after putting so much time and money into the condo, we found a big Victorian home with a wrap-around porch in the Arverne section of Far Rockaway. The house was everything we wanted. So we signed a contract to buy it.

In 2011 weather forecasters did a great job of scaring the Rockaway Beach community about the encroaching Hurricane Irene. People scrambled to buy generators. They stocked up on food. They boarded up their businesses and homes. But in the end the storm passed through the Rockaways with little excitement. So when forecasters again warned us of the possible dangers of Hurricane Sandy in 2012, the community remained indifferent. Another Irene, we thought. But for safe measure I nailed some two-by-fours across the glass front of the gym. Then Sarah, Jube, Gio, and I waited out the storm in our condo.

As the storm neared the shores of Rockaway Beach, we—along with the entire northeastern corridor of the United States—knew this wasn't going to be another Irene. The winds blew stronger. The rain pelted harder. The waves crested higher. Rockaway Beach officials mandated an evacuation. But I wasn't ready to throw in the towel yet. I felt a sense of duty to stick around and hold down what was ours. But the storm grew more intense and Sarah's good judgment kicked in. We packed a few things and left everything behind, not knowing what we'd return to.

We went to my parent's house in Queens Village because it was safer for the kids while the storm rolled through. And from my parent's living room Sarah and I watched on TV as Hurricane Sandy tore up Rockaway Beach. News reporters stood sideways on the boardwalk while reporting. Police officers climbed to the roof of the precinct to escape the flooding. Cars floated down the streets. The reports were coming in that Rockaway Beach was under eight to ten feet of water. Sarah and I tried to keep the faith. Maybe we were one of the lucky ones. Maybe the water didn't touch our condo or gym. But then the TV station cut away to a shot of Ninety-Second Street, in front of CROM gym. And the entire area was underwater. I looked over at Sarah, and I could see in her face she was trying to hold herself together in front of my mom and Jube. Sarah put her head on the table and broke down. I took her into my arms. "We're gonna come back bigger and better," I said.

Truth be told, I didn't know how we'd come back. But I believed if we stayed in each other's corner we'd bounce back. I made an entire career off of comebacks. And not too long after Sarah and I were married, I coached Sarah for and through her first boxing match. Sarah showed me her own determination after her opponent hit her with a body hook that temporarily halted Sarah. She went on to win the fight. And we walked away with a strong belief in ourselves as a couple. I had no doubts we'd rise up alongside each other after Sandy.

A few days passed before Rockaway Beach officials let us back in to assess the damage at home, at the gym, and in the community. We didn't know what to expect, but as we neared Rockaway we took in the aftermath. Our first obstacle was getting into Rockaway Beach. We couldn't get across the Cross Bay Veterans Memorial Bridge because a fifty-foot boat washed up on Cross Bay Boulevard. We navigated the back roads, maneuvering through the destruction. Giant chunks of boardwalk rested in front of houses and lodged themselves into cars. And cars teetered one on top of the next. On street corners bulldozers piled tons of sand, which blanketed everything the ocean waters touched.

We couldn't drive to the gym because the streets were still flooded. So Sarah and I parked a few blocks away and, with flashlight in hand, trekked through sewage and seawater toward the gym. From the outside looking in, I couldn't tell how much damage the gym took. And I didn't have anything to pry off the two-by-fours. Sarah and I went around back and I peeled open the rear door.

The smell hit me first. The air reeked of sewage and mold and hopelessness. Even though the waters receded the devastation remained. Everything the ocean swallowed was ruined. Sheetrock hung off the beams. Furniture sat upside down. The ring was the only thing intact. Building the ring took us three days, thanks to our student, Mike Saperstein, who we called The Roofmaster. He was a welder by trade. And because the gym was small we had to connect the ring ropes to the wall using metal plates and rings. So he showed me a thing or two about welding. I felt accomplished using my hands for something other than punching. During our first smoker, though, the ropes couldn't withstand the weight of the fighters' bodies and they sagged under the pressure. But there the ropes were, after the storm, still hanging on.

About eight feet off the ground, hanging from the brick wall, was the CROM Gym flag. I wore it into the ring since my first pro fight. In the middle of the flag was the sun from the Filipino flag, and my motto, "All it takes is heart." I admired the famous western Muay Thai fighter, Danny Bill. He made his entrance to the ring with a cape-style robe. So I adopted the style and used my gym flag to represent my mission as a fighter, because battle campaigns require a battle flag. And most of my opponents were from out of town; I wanted them to know they were coming to claim my territory. After Sandy, midway up the length of the flag there was a waterline. The ocean might've taken most of our territory, but it didn't take everything.

Our condo suffered much of the same damage. Sarah and I walked into the first floor of the condo and the familiar smell of mold and sewage hung in the air. The only thing salvageable was the washing machine. The basement was dark and cold and the air felt toxic. Sludge covered everything. The three hundred dollar TV stand sat on its side with games pouring out of the drawers. The flood destroyed Jube's clothes and sneaker collection. The only clothes he had left were the shirt and pants he was wearing.

But we still had enough to hold onto. We spent close to three years immersing ourselves in Rockaway Beach. We didn't want to turn our backs on the community when they needed us most. And our students also needed us. But more importantly, Sarah and I needed each other, because ahead of us, the greatest comeback of our lives awaited.

The help came from home first. And, like the storm itself, reached a far greater area than our Rockaway Beach community. In the days and weeks after Hurricane Sandy, my mother let Sarah, the kids, and me stay in her house while we cleaned out the condo. My mom cooked us warm meals and looked after Gio and Jube as Sarah and I figured out how to get back on our feet. Help poured in from the Muay Thai community next.

Sean Hinds came out from East Harlem to help us clean out our condo. Sarah's friend, who was also helping us, didn't know anything about Muay Thai and found out Sean and I were both fighters. "Wouldn't it be cool if you guys fought each other on a charity show to raise money to rebuild the gym?" her friend said. Sean George also came out from C3 Gym in Connecticut. I never shared the ring or a word with him until that day. When I saw him hop out of his truck with crutches and a cast, I knew he had a big heart. "I'm a big fan of your fighting," he said. He had manpower, tools, food, and water.

Not long after the storm, Kevin Murphy also reached out to us. And he contacted his network of people. And the donations poured in. And once word spread the help continued. People from Coban's gym, North Jersey Muay Thai, Pittsburgh Muay Thai, and more offered their time and donations. On the West Coast, Chaz Mulkey and Joe Schilling reached out to express their sympathy and they organized a fundraiser to help us out. Our student, John Rullan, came with a truck and helped clean up. There was a shortage of gasoline in the five boroughs, and we were eating up a lot of gas driving back and forth from Rockaway to Queens Village. One of Coban's students, Jay Marist, drove upstate and bought us containers of gasoline, lasting us a few weeks.

Coban and his wife, Sandra, organized a seminar that Coban and I taught at his gym. I trained with Coban in the past as a student, but to share the floor with one of the greatest fighters in Muay Thai history as a coach was an honor. In the end, Coban and

Sandra donated the proceeds to us to help rebuild our gym and presented us with a generous gift card to Title Boxing.

Take On promotions, organized by Aziz Nabih and Eddie Cuello, held a raffle at their Madison Square Garden event and sent the proceeds our way. And Justin Blair organized a Friday Night Fights charity event with the proceeds going to help us rebuild our lives. At the end of the night I stepped into the ring to thank the crowd. "Hurricane Sandy is a lot like fighting," I said. "We got put down for an eight count, but we're gonna pick ourselves back up and fight harder until the end." Steve Ferdman, long-time fight photographer for Friday Night Fights, organized a t-shirt fundraiser with Dan Dejos of Artlete. The shirt was printed with "We Storm Back."

The way the community came together during Sandy was amazing. But even with the help pouring in our lives forever changed. When we lost the gym we lost our means of income. My best friend, Gabe, let us live in his basement for almost six months. And Natalie Fuz from Chok Sabai Gym let me use her gym to train my clients. With the help of Cyrus Washington, Tyrone Cunningham from Militia Muay Thai let me teach a few classes per week at their gym. I traveled all over the place to stay involved in any way I could.

I taught full-time at CROM Martial Training for two years before Sandy hit. I didn't want my students thinking we bailed on them during the hardest times. I was grateful people from the Muay Thai community allowed me to work from their gyms. But I knew I had to get back to Rockaway to continue building up what Sarah and I started. And in January of 2013, we took our Muay Thai gear—donated by EVERLAST with the help of Erik Naranjo—and began teaching at the local Knights of Columbus. We gave free gloves to anyone who lost them in Sandy. And two days a week we crammed our gear into our '06 Subaru Forester and taught classes under the chandelier on the dance floor.

Our life was in such chaos we weren't sure of our next move at times. We knew we wanted to continue teaching Muay Thai. We knew we wanted to rebuild our gym. We knew we wanted to stay in Rockaway. So we moved into an apartment next to the Knights of Columbus. And when time permitted, we trained our students—J.C. included—in our living room. In the meantime Sarah and I looked for a new place to open CROM Martial Training. And to our surprise, the Rockaway Wave, the local newspaper that lost their production gear to Sandy, let us rent their two thousand square foot space. We hung up sheetrock, threw down some mats, and called the space home for the next six months.

But getting our students back was challenging. Most of our students moved out of Rockaway, some for higher ground, some because their homes burnt to the ground. And let's face it; many students didn't have the money or ambition to train. They'd lost everything. And like us they had to rebuild their own lives. Sandy might've taken away many of our members, but over time we rebuilt our gym. We welcomed old members back and we welcomed new members in.

Sandy and the rebuilding process have shown me that the fight to become more, to become better, never ends. We must battle everyday of our lives, whether we're fighting for something big or something small. And fights, no matter how big or how small, require us to dig deep and scrap hard, because anything worth having on this journey through life doesn't come easily. And what's acquired easily comes and goes the same. So I take solace knowing fighting has never come easy for me, knowing that relationships have never come easy for me, and knowing that fatherhood has never come easy for me. Knowing this reminds me that I need to fight for these things most.

When we moved to Rockaway Beach Sarah and I wanted a home. But we got a community. Sarah and I wanted a place to raise Jube and Gio. But we got the challenge of raising ourselves, raising ourselves up from the hardest knockdown life has ever hit us with. I joke around that I was born, raised, and trapped in Queens. And over the years, I felt in many ways I never made a name for myself outside of New York. But the truth is, I was created, molded, and made stronger by Queens. And even though I never traveled or fought as much as I would've liked to outside of New York, when the help poured in from across America, I realized just how far the Romulo name had taken me.

POST-FIGHT ANALYSIS

EPILOGUE
CHAMPIONS UPRISING

*"Everything I was I carry with me, everything I will be lies waiting on
the road ahead."*
- Ma Jian

After Sandy and during the rebuilding process our lives were chaotic. But Sarah and I rose back to our feet and rebuilt our gym, CROM Martial Training. And ten years after winning my own amateur state and national titles, three of the six fighters who I took to the 2014 WKAs won national titles of their own. During the same time Sarah and I started our own amateur Muay Thai promotion in Rockaway, called Battle Rock. We promoted four shows, which featured some of the best amateur fighters from the eastern seaboard. And later on in 2014, I brought two fighters to the WKA World Championships in Tuscany, Italy, and two of them brought home the silver.

In 2016 I also hosted the first ever World Muay Thai Summit. The summit took place online and featured conversations with some of Muay Thai's biggest names, such as Rob Cox, John Wayne Parr, Ognjen Topic, and Joseph Valtellini—to name a few. Altogether, twenty people from all walks of life talked about what brought them to Muay Thai, their histories in the sport, and how the martial art has shaped their lives.

And in late 2016 I made my first trip back to Thailand since I fought at the IFMAs in 2004. The trip was part of a social media project sponsored by Chang Beer, the Striking Corner Podcast, and Tourism Authority of Thailand. For two weeks, Sarah, Gio, and I went to six different gyms in Bangkok and Hua Hin and highlighted each of them, their fighters, and their coaches.

With fatherhood, though, the challenge continues. But so does the learning. And everyday I'm learning how to adapt. When my first son, Jube, was born, he saved my life. Jube gave me the opportunity to break the cycle of non-existent fathers in my family. Because he was with me from the beginning of my journey, I have faith he'll take with him through life the lessons I've passed along, whether through action or words. Jube is now nineteen years old. He's dealing with the struggles of finding his own uprising. And although we have our differences of opinion, I'm doing my best to let him find his own way as a man. And although he hasn't chosen to follow me as a fighter, the last time we put the gloves on he nearly took my head off. When Jube was a kid I introduced him as my bodyguard. And since I'm still here today to tell this story, I would say he did a great job.

My younger son, Gio, is now five years old. He was born and raised in our newest gym, CROM Physical Culture. He loves Brazilian Jiu Jitsu, boxing, and burpees. And I love to see him involved with something Sarah and I have invested our lives into. When Sarah and I decide to retire on a secluded beach in an undisclosed location, Gio will probably be the one to take over the family business.

My relationship with my own father has improved as well. After fifty years, he had a reunion with his long-lost younger brother, and my father has since opened up. And when we greet each other there is more than the usual "head-nod" hello. We shook hands and had our first ever hug. I have no more ill feelings toward my father and at seventy-eight years of age, I wish him a happy and joyous life. Looking back, I would not change a thing between us, because our relationship has blessed me with the character I need for the rest of my journey.

My championship pursuit still continues, although my focus has shifted from the ring to the gym, from fighter to coach. I now live through those I teach. I see in my young students so much of who I was, and because I know where they can bring themselves with a little nudge, I invest myself in them like a father. And I also see a lot of myself in my adult students, because each of them is trying to shed an old part of themselves and replace it with who they could become. And I am at the same point in my life, once again.

My mission now is to take what I've overcome on the streets of Queens, what I've learned over the years in the ring and in the gym, and spread the message to the masses through my C.H.A.M.P.S. U.P.R.I.S.E. Program and public speaking. I suppose, in a way, public speaking is the closest I'll ever get to fighting again. And just as I used fighting to show people how to overcome life's challenges, I want to use public speaking to do the same. Because life will knock you down seven times, but you have to stand up eight. We all have a champion in us fighting to win at life. Champ up.

ACKNOWLEDGEMENTS

Thank you to my children and wife for being my rocks in life. I'm not only strong for them, but I'm strong through them. Life will always test our bonds. And I look forward to every pebble, crack, or bump we'll stumble upon. I know deep in my heart I'm a family man, even though there was a time when I thought otherwise. Family is what you make of it, so I choose not to live out of my past, but to live out of my imagination.

Thank you to the Romulo family for supporting me through the dark times and always guiding me toward the light.

Thank you to the entire Gregory family for supporting our dreams and visions.

Thank you to my coaches at CROM PC for inspiring me everyday, allowing me to keep growing and keep reaching for the top!

Thank you to my students past and present, from young lions to more experienced fighters, for trusting me while starting your own journey through the world of Muay Thai.

Thank you to my clients and gym members past and present who have helped me become the coach that I've always wanted to be.

Thank you to my coaches, mentors, and training partners who took the time to share what they've learned with me.

Thank you to my opponents who stepped in the ring with me and risked it all to experience what true passion and love is about.

Thank you to my supporters across the globe that have never met me in person but allow me to share my world with them.

Thank you to our Rockaway Beach Community for adopting us. (I've still never been referred to as a Hipster to this day so I think they might really like us.)

Thank you to everyone that supported us with donations, hard work, and just plain old kindness during and after Sandy.

Thank you to the entire NYC Muay Thai community for having open eyes, ears, and minds for the art we love.

Thank you to Friday Night Fights for giving me a place to paint the perfect picture.

Thank you to Lion Fight for giving me an opportunity to fight outside of my hometown.

Thank you to Church Street Boxing Gym for giving Jube and me a place to call home during the "Feudal Era."

Thank you to New York Sports Club for giving me a place to rebuild the life that I now embrace.

Thank you to Fairtex San Francisco and Banphli for testing my love for the Art of 8 Limbs.

Thank you to the Seaport Fight Crew for opening my eyes and guiding me to become a well-rounded martial artist.

Thank you to the Tommy Thai Team. When a sword is first being forged it starts out as an ugly, unrefined piece of metal. It's nothing remotely close to a weapon that can be used for structured battle. But when it's heated and pounded over and over it can be sharpened and polished for victory. In the short amount of time that I spent with Tommy and the fellas, they were the final pound from the hammer before I set off to be tested thereafter.

Thank you to everyone on Two Hundred and Eighth Street in The Ville for raising me through the Golden Era of childhood. We had no clue what awaited us, but we marched on with faith that brighter days were ahead. Those days defined The Thick and Thin of life. And although each of us has chosen our own paths as adults, I'll never forget all that was said and done to help outgrow The Ville. It was the place where we started our journeys, and even though we've left, it will forever be a part of us, pushing us through and further along our journeys through life.

Thank you to Edwin. There are many teachers that I've come across on my journey, teachers who've shown me valuable things about fighting and life. But Edwin taught me the most crucial lesson of all, to always ask the question, "Why are you here?"

And last but not least, thank you to John Wolcott. From the first time we crossed paths and I read his work, I had a feeling that he could relate to where I'd been. Though we are worlds apart in most ways, we are still the same, same. We know the purpose to life is more than just existing, it's truly living. I've once again trusted someone with fewer years than me on this planet, believing in his passion to help me with the only thing I'll bring to the end of days—my story.

ABOUT THE AUTHORS

Chris Romulo runs CROM Physical Culture in Rockaway Beach, NY where he lives with his wife, Sarah, and two sons, Jube and Giovanni. For speaking engagements, you can reach Chris at www.ChrisRomulo.com.

John Wolcott is a freelance writer and lives in Bangkok, Thailand with his wife, Mallika, and their two daughters, Makayla and Nova. You can reach John at www.JohnWolcott.com.

To view photos of Chris Romulo's life inside and outside of the ring, please visit www.ChrisRomulo.com/memories.

And while you're there, download the Champ Up MP3 to help you win at life.

Made in the USA
Middletown, DE
25 May 2017